My Vision of Hell

(A Sacrifice for Others to See)

Proverbs 3:5+6; Trust in the Lord with all thine heart, and lean not unto thine own understanding. In all thy ways acknowledge Him, and He shall direct thy paths. God Bless!!

Pastor Sheila M. Drummer

P.S.Drummer
6/8/2023

ISBN 978-1-64458-973-1 (paperback)
ISBN 978-1-64458-974-8 (digital)

Copyright © 2019 by Pastor Sheila M. Drummer

All rights reserved. No part of this publication may be reproduced, distributed, or transmitted in any form or by any means, including photocopying, recording, or other electronic or mechanical methods without the prior written permission of the publisher. For permission requests, solicit the publisher via the address below.

Christian Faith Publishing, Inc.
832 Park Avenue
Meadville, PA 16335
www.christianfaithpublishing.com

All Scripture quotations in this book are from the King James Version of the Bible.

Printed in the United States of America

Dedications

First, I dedicate this book to God, my Heavenly Father, his son Jesus, my Savior, and his Holy Spirit, who has given me wisdom and strength throughout the completion of his testimony. He showed me mercy, love, understanding and knowledge during the process of this writing. Thank you, Father, for helping me to realize just how much you love me. Thank you for entrusting me with this message of urgency to your people in your churches, everywhere.

Secondly, I dedicate this writing to my husband Michael, who has been there patiently supporting me to get this writing done. I thank God for you!

I further dedicate this writing to every one of my children: Kimberly, Michael II, Angela, Donna, Steven, Christopher and Wesley. You all have carried my vision in your hearts from the day you all were able to understand. I pray that you will each receive and apply all the teachings that God has given me as I have learned of him throughout this process; having learned that hell, it is a real place. It is further, my prayer, that with the knowledge contained herein these pages, you will all miss it (HELL)!

Finally, to my grandchildren, my mom, my siblings, aunts, uncles, nieces, nephews, cousins and in-laws, and to God's people everywhere, I pray that you will each receive and apply all the teachings that God has given me as I have learned of him throughout this process; having learned that hell, it is a real place. It is further, my prayer, that with the knowledge contained herein these pages, you will all miss it (HELL)!

Acknowledgements

I thank God for my husband Michael of thirty-seven years and counting, our seven children, and seventeen grandchildren and counting. I thank all my family and friends who kept me encouraged during this process, may God continue to Bless you all.

And to my Pastors, John and Bonnie (Althea) Turner, who has kept me in constant prayer in ministry work and throughout the years, especially in the completion of this project, God bless you both, your family, and the Blessing Corner Ministries family.

To Dr. Larry V. Houston, thank you for applying your God-given talent, when you took on the daunting task for the much-needed editorial services for this writing. With your talents, you have allowed me to better express the thoughts of my heart without taking away from my God-given message. You are truly, truly a blessing, and I pray God's continued blessings upon your family and all your future endeavors.

Lastly, to Mother Bobbie Turner, thank you for being the prayer warrior needed along the way, God bless you!

Table of Contents

Introduction 9

The Writings 15

Seeing with My Eyes, Hearing with my Ears 32

Getting in the Fight 42

My Vision of Hell Unfolds by God 46

My Prayer and My Song 53

Innocence Taken, But God 59

The Closing 67

Introduction

My Vision of Hell: A Sacrifice for Others to See is a dream that God gave to me at the beginning of 1992. By the end of that same year, I had fallen into a backslidden condition. After a period of repentance, in 1995, God gave me the order in which he wanted me to write about it.

It was such a struggle for me to even start writing, because, regrettably, I backslid again in 1996. I realized that this job was not for me, and I knew that God had definitely chosen the wrong person to write for him.

There was so much I wanted to say in this book, but God held my tongue. In 1997, not feeling worthy to even repent, I asked God to please deliver me from these personal lusts and strongholds that kept me going backwards—backwards into the very things I did not want to do, but I could not stop myself from doing (Romans 7:15–25).

Over the next five years, I sought God's face continuously, crying out and asking him to forgive me and for him to help me in everything and in every way to change. I could not forgive myself. I prayed and said:

"Father God in Jesus's name, please forgive me. I need your shed blood and your death on the cross through Jesus Christ. I need it to work for me. Please, come into my heart and mind all over again and even come into the particles of my flesh that make up my body, if possible. Lord, God, please, help me to overcome. I can't do this myself, because I truly want you to tell me when I stand before you on that day, 'Well done, thou good and faithful servant' (Matthew 25:21). Father, I believe that Jesus died on the cross for all my sins, and I know that they are many. Father God, I pray this prayer in the name of Jesus."

I cannot recall the day, but in December 2003, God audibly spoke in my ears, "I've called imperfect people for perfect tasks" (1 Corinthians 1:27–29). At that same moment, something happened in my heart, and I felt different. It was as if he had forgiven my fall in 1996 too. He didn't even bring it up or say anything about my failures. He went on to tell me what it will take to make it with him. Then, that sweet voice of Jesus started to give me all kinds of scriptures, teaching me, through the Bible, the Word of God. He also ensured me that within him (Jesus) are great victories (1 John 5:4). All the scriptures that he gave me are written in this book. I didn't know where to begin writing, so I prayed and asked God to please pen this book, because I'm not a writer. I became obedient in studying his word as he told me (2 Timothy 2:15). As a result, the words of the Bible began to become alive in my heart and mind, and I was able to actually see what God was saying. Every scripture was as if it was a parable I could now understand (Mark 4:10–13).

Then, one day, he just began to speak all these words into my mind. The words began to form so quickly that I had to get a pencil and paper to write everything down as he was revealing it to me. As he spoke words into my mind, I saw my notebook forming "My Vision of Hell" before my eyes. He gave me so much wisdom, because I knew that I could not have thought of all these things by myself.

Prior to this awakening, I had read and studied the Bible from Genesis to Revelation, and I thought I understood what God's word was saying. I truly thought that I was saved. I thought I was already obeying God's word. I thought that I was really living for him, but as God brought me out of this sinful state, it was Jesus who taught me what it really meant to be Christlike and what it will take to be a true believer, living in God's word, the Bible (1 John 4:9). Jesus taught me all over again! I have found out that it's not enough only for one to believe in God; one must become a doer of his holy word (James 1:22–23).

Oh, how God loves his church (his people). God told me to write this book, because he wanted his people to know that hell is real, and I wanted you to know that you can make it if you only dare to believe that Jesus is the Christ, the one and only begotten son of God (1 Peter 1:18–25; 1 John 2:23, 5:10). In other words, there wasn't anyone before like *Jesus*, neither will there be anyone after like *Jesus* (Acts 4:12)! He's the only true Savior that came to redeem us from our sins and that God's holy word [the Bible] is the final authority by which we must be saved and live (Hebrews 10).

Jesus die once for all persons, and his death on the cross is the answer for every situation we may encounter in life. We have to form a personal relationship with God through his son, Jesus Christ. We must believe in his dying on the cross and that his resurrection from the dead has satisfied the payment of death for our sins (Ephesians 2). Consequently, Christ has brought you and I into a relationship, not into a religion, with our heavenly father. This is what the whole Bible is based on: Jesus. Therefore, God sent us a Savior, because we could not and cannot save ourselves (John 3:16).

God wants us to live a life that is saved, healthy, and in prosperity (3 John 1:2). He wants us to surrender our will to his will (the word of God). This is one of the hardest things for any person to do, but it can be accomplished in the Lord. It does not mean that everything will be smooth sailing either. Jesus said "These things I have spoken unto you, that in me ye might have peace. In the world ye shall have tribulation: but be of good cheer; I have overcome the world" (John 16:33).

However, I have found out that true repentance means that one is willing to make a change and turn away, with the help of the Lord Jesus from sinful ways, so that the spirit of lust or whatever the strongholds are in your life, may be broken or destroyed. Without deliverance by the Spirit of God, you will always find yourself going back and forth to that _____ [you fill in the blank], believing the lie that 'it will be better the next time'. (James 1:13-16, Revelation 2:5)

This can happen only by accepting Jesus Christ, God's son, as your personal Lord and Savior and believing that Jesus' death and resurrection is God's only prescription for us to be delivered and set free from the bondages of sin. God showed me how his word is better than medicine, even surgery (Proverbs 3:1–2, 8 and Hebrews 4:12). We must take it [medicine] as prescribed by the doctor for whatever symptoms we may have. If we don't follow the doctor's orders, we will not get well; we will become sicker. It's the same with the word of God. Again, this is God's only plan for reconciling us (man) back to himself (Colossians 1:20–29). All paths do not lead to God as many believe. However, God did say he will direct our paths (Psalms 23:2-3, 25:4–10, 37:23; Proverbs 3:5–6).

If anyone tries to get to God [heaven] any other way except through *Jesus*, they will fail and miss heaven altogether (John 14:6). Jesus said, "I am the way, the truth, and the life, no man cometh to the father [go to heaven], but by me [Jesus]."

Jesus said "No man can come to me, except the Father which hath sent me draw him: and I will raise him up at the last day. (John 6:44)

There are so many writings now on divine revelations of heaven and/or hell that I purposely did not read any of them, because I did not want what God had told me or had shown to me to be influenced by someone else's experience. My spiritual journey has been a hard one, day in and day out, especially gaining back the trust of my Lord and Savior Jesus Christ. So, I can only imagine how hard it must have been for many around me to open their hearts and trust me once again to handle the precious word of God. But to God be the glory. He fixed it all. Glory, hallelujah (2 Corinthians 4).

In 1998, I received my ministerial license, and God raised me up to be the assistant youth pastor of a thriving ministry in Bakersfield, California, called Greater Lighthouse Community Outreach, Inc., d/b/a The Blessing Comer Ministries under the leadership of copastors John and Althea (Bonnie) Turner, who were ordained pastors in 1996. The pastors would have me to come up and tell my testimony as the Holy Spirit would lead them in the services at our church. Just like in times past and even up to now, when I would tell my testimony, the spirit of God is still drawing many souls to the altar in repentance. I am very grateful to God to see the many souls that are saved, as they are drawn by the Holy Spirit. I am always encouraged by my pastors to continue telling the vision of my visit to hell and how God let me come back to tell about it. By the grace of God, I've been going over twenty years strong for the Lord. My husband and I celebrated our thirty-seventh wedding anniversary last August 2018.

As it was with Joseph in Genesis 50:20: whatever the evil was that was against me, God has now meant it for my good, to bring to pass, as it is this day, to save much people alive. To God be all the glory, thanks and praise for what He has done and for what He is going to do.

The Writings

Twice in 1992, God, through and by his precious Holy Spirit, gave me the same dreams of warning where he took me to hell. Six months later, I completely backslid. Shortly thereafter, the same dream returned, but this time, it was far more intense. Although I have shared my dreams in testimony at a few churches, and I often share it in my home church, I found myself still being out of God's will, because I had not completely done what he had asked me to do with the visions of hell until now. I have *completed* my book. All praises be to God, my heavenly father!

At the time, I often thought to myself, *Why is God letting me go to hell in dreams? Why would he let me see such a place, such a horrible place?*

For months after my dreams, I was tormented and scared with the thoughts and vivid memories of what I had seen. There were so many nights of lost sleep from my fears of falling back into the same dreams of going to hell. I tried my best to appear normal in my everyday life, as I refrained from telling anyone about the dream, because I did not want anyone to know what God had showed me.

Hell was a topic that was taught very often in our little church, and I would say to myself, *If I told this, people would think I was hell bound for sure.*

So since I didn't want to wear that label, I simply kept my dreams to myself and decided that I'm not telling anyone (Job 7:13–15)!

During the time of my dreams, our family members were faithful to the church we attended in Watts, California; I was working as a full-time volunteer. The church had multiple outreach programs that addressed the many needs of individuals in the surrounding Los

Angeles communities. It was an honor to be a part of such a great work. I became so involved in the ministry's work that I was elevated to the position of office manager of this outreach that fed up to fifty thousand people per month. In addition, I served as a Sunday school teacher, member of the prayer team and the choir, and one of the leaders of praise and worship. I was also a part of our church's gospel-singing group that traveled across the country and participated in various music workshops sponsored by such personalities as Dr. Bobby Jones and the late Rev. James Cleveland. I was participating in nearly every part of the ministry. The more I worked, the less I would think about the dreams that God had given me. I kept myself so busy with church activities that I got to the place where I wasn't thinking about the dreams at all.

I was so busy being involved in everything at our church until I did not see the enemy coming. Because of my position, I had to interact with everyone who worked in our outreach program. Therefore, I began to overextend myself which accelerated my downfall. By the end of 1992, I had slowed down in the areas of my constant fasting and prayer. It seemed like if and when I'd fast or prayed, I was doing it wrong or for the wrong reasons. I then began to fall in my Christian walk, although my complete fall did not happen overnight. I spent months trying to fight against the thoughts that had formed in my mind and the desires that had formed in my heart. I tried so hard to get back on track and to work things out on my own through fasting and praying to God. Though I was asking him to help me, it was as if my desires just overtook my flesh. I was like a yoyo—going up and down, up and down. Yet and still, I know that God was answering my prayers with the help that I needed, because I would stand strong for many months at a time, but I would always gravitate right back into my failures. I learned in the scriptures that God gives his people a way of escape so as not to commit sin (1 Corinthians 10:13; Revelation 2:4–5). He would let the phone ring, or a knock would come at the door right at the very moment of temptation, or he would even speak to you. That is how He got my attention to stop me from actually sinning! I remember God saying to me, "Don't do that," as I made plans to go and sin. However, since I ignored his sweet voice of warning, sin entered into my heart even before I had committed the actual acts. I later learned from God's word that just the thought of going against his word took me out of his will. Then, the desires to do wrong came (James 1:13–15). Yes, I backslid.

After I backslid in 1993, months later, one night, God allowed me to fall back into the same dream. This time, however, it was more intense than ever. The order of the dream did not change from what I had seen the first two times, but this time, the dream was more detailed and intense (Isaiah 55:11). God started taking the dream and my whole life apart simultaneously. It was so that I could understand the importance of his words to me and having eternal life through Jesus Christ, his son.

Within this written testimony, I wanted to detail all my failures and promiscuous acts that had caused me to fall. I kept falling back into sin before Jesus rescued me. I didn't want to keep anything back from you, but God said to me, "I know, and those who were there, they know for sin is sin in my sight, no matter what the sin or who you are."

I thought about that statement for a long time, and although I still felt as if I were keeping a secret from you, the reader, God still said, "No, for all unrighteousness is sin" (1 John 5:17–21).

I'm somewhat glad that he told me not to reveal them. I'm pleased about this not because I would be ashamed or embarrassed but because if I should get a chance to tell my testimony in your church or city, I would not want you to be distracted. I'm now forgiven (Roman 6, 1 John 1:9–10)

God spoke to me and said, "Write it down and put it in a book. Tell my Churches… (Tell my People)…Hell…It…Is…Real!" (Habakkuk 2:2–4; Revelations 22:16)!

When the matter was brought to the senior pastor, he immediately called me to his office to discuss the situation. He started by asking me to sit down, and I did. Then, he said, "Little Sheila, some disturbing news has been brought to me, and I need to find out if it is true or not, so I can straighten out the lies that are being spread in the church about you."

I sat there quietly, as he rubbed his chin, and then, he asked me, "Sheila, were you a part of this?"

Still, I remained quiet and did not respond, knowing that I was at a defining moment to face what I had done. In this moment of truth, I was gripped with shame and utter embarrassment, so I choose not to confess that I was a part of it. I boldly lied (while smiling), as I said to him, "No, Pastor, what you have heard about me wasn't the truth."

After I said that, I felt something left me, I felt numb on the inside, and I didn't feel good in my heart. God must have revealed to him that I was lying. He began to tell me about the time that God had become angry with his sister and wouldn't allow him to pray for her either. God was now allowing him to feel the same way toward me. He then asked me again if I had sinned, and after that, I could not hold it in any more. I broke down and cried saying, "Yes, yes, I have. I have sinned."

He told me, "Ask God to forgive you, because he won't let me pray with you."

From that moment on, I knew what it was that I felt. It was God's displeasure; although his presence (the Holy Spirit) was in the room. He surrounded me with warmth, and the warmness felt like an atmosphere for the truth. I knew that everything I had to say from that point on had to be the truth. It was as if God was so very angry with me for lying. It would have been much better for me to have told the truth no matter the consequences. As I sat in that office chair with my head down and arms crossed crying, I felt like a little child standing before my parents who already knew the truth; but I had just told them a boldface lie.

I don't think God would be displeased if I address the following passage to his pastors:

> *Now, I know how disappointing it is to a pastor who truly preaches and teaches the gospel, the cross, and to have one of his or her members to fall from grace; in some part, that pastor feels the hurt right along with the fallen. If you are a pastor, I beseech you that you continue preaching the uncompromised word of God and give space for having altar calls.*

> *Do not fall away from sound doctrine (Titus 1:9, 2:1 and 1 Corinthians 2:2). We cannot compromise the word of God (Acts 5:29, 1 Corinthians 9:14, Mark 1:4, Luke 4:17–19, Romans 1:16, 10:15, 1 Corinthians 1:17–23, and 2 Timothy 4:2).*
>
> *Please seek God fervently for the full understanding of these passages as well, and then, teach it to your parishioners because you are God's watchman.*
>
> *Hebrews 13:17 states, "Obey them that have the rule over you and submit yourselves for they watch for your souls, as they that must give account, that they may do it with joy, and not with grief, for that is unprofitable for you."*
>
> *As followers of Christ and leaders, we are made accountable of the word and the work and must sit down and count up the cost (Luke 14:28–33). We must trust and depend on God to help us finish this great work of his, which is to preach about Jesus and him crucified (1 Corinthians 2:2).*
>
> *The pastors are God's watchmen (Ezekiel 3:17–21). Every church has one. That God sent man or woman is also going to be held accountable for every single person (every soul) sitting under his or her ministry (Romans 10:14-15).*

I realized I did not only hurt God who trusted me with the handling of his word but my pastors who always preached to me about loving God and living free from sin. For, they truly watched over my soul and taught me God's word. Also, I failed the members who trusted in me; but I broke their trust and let them down as well.

Several days after talking to the pastor and having admitted my sins, I was downstairs in the outreach office, hard at work, when the pastor asked me up to his office once again. As I arrived and sat down, he said to me, "Sheila we have to relieve you of all of your duties, and we need you to turn in all of your keys for the church and outreach. We (pastor and the first lady) feel that you need to take time to seek God for your salvation for that's far more important for you right now than for you to continue working in the ministry."

Then, they asked me, "Why did you lie? God was trying to help you to come clean out of the situation" (1 John 1:9–10).

I then replied to them, "I was ashamed. I was too ashamed," and truly I was. After that meeting, whatever they said to me, I did and accepted without question. I didn't fight against any of their decisions.

In the long run, I decided not to leave the church. As I evaluated my situation (having truly repented and desiring to be fully restored in God), I thought, *Why should I leave the church where God had set me* (1 Corinthians 12:18 and Proverbs 25:27)? *How can I leave God to go and try to find Him somewhere else?*

The situation would still be there against me no matter where I went. No, I realized that I messed up here and have accepted that fact. Now, God is giving me the chance to choose life or death eternally (heaven or hell). I became one hundred percent obedient to my pastor and church leaders who God had placed over me as they continued to watch for my soul.

For the next two and a half years, God sat me down in the ministry. I attended services only and no longer took an active part in any auxiliaries in the church. I had lied greatly in God's face by denying my sins; I had hurt so many brothers and sisters in the church who trusted me in my position of trust and authority. The next person I hurt was my dear husband. I prayed daily that he would forgive me which he has and thank God because God is a God of reconciliation. During this time, our children were too young to understand.

I really had to depend on God to help me as I obeyed his will in writing this book, because I had not written down any dates when he would tell me things. I could remember him telling me something one week. Then, weeks, if not months, would pass before hearing a word from God again. Although I continued in prayer daily, I don't remember how long of a period it was that God continued to deal with me in this manner. Meanwhile, as I was praying one evening, God told me to study (2 Timothy 2:15) and search the scriptures to learn of him (John 5:39). I had faced the truth within myself that I had sinned. I began to study and search the scriptures from 1993 to 1995 without a break. This helped me develop discipline for researching the Bible today. I was disciplined and obedient to God's leading with my studying. As I studied, God would talk to my mind by telling me things about myself in his word (Proverbs 1:23-31). The Bible became a living mirror for my life to reflect from (1 Corinthians 13:12; 2 Corinthians 3:18). I saw myself as a sinner before God almighty, destined for hell from the church (Psalms 1:1–6 and Revelation 3:14–22).

However, I've also experienced his grace and mercy toward me, giving me a chance to change my ways (Romans 12:1–2; Hebrews 10:16–22; 1 John 2:15–17).

Today, I am forgiven and living a saved life by the grace of God through my faith in what Jesus did for me on the cross. I knew then that it was essential for me to know God for myself (John 14:21, 23–24). I needed to accept him for who he truly is and what he is to me and to conform to what he will accept and will not accept (Proverbs 6:16–19). Most importantly, God told me to study and learn of him (Isaiah 54:13).

I was one of those individuals who thought that God and I had an understanding. I would tell myself, *All I had to do was to repent after I had purposely planned and carried out my sins. After all, God is going to forgive me, because I'm highly favored.* How foolish to think that God would go against his word for me while living in sin, He could have chosen anyone to do what he wants done.

I was looking at what a few other people were doing in the church, because I was completely aware of their actions. I thought, *Well, if they are doing what they want to do (and God seems to be forgiving them and seems to be blessing them), then why can't I have fun too? After all, all I have to do is to ask Jesus to forgive me.*

Well, God gave me a very rude awakening.

Month after month, service after service, even in my own private prayer time after my pastors had confronted me about the situation and I lied, I could no longer feel the presence of God's Holy Spirit. My joy was gone; there was no peace left in my troubled heart. I started feeling this hurting in my heart that would not go away. It was there all the time, aching me beyond what words could ever describe. It was a pain I had never felt before or would ever want anyone else to ever experience. As I endured living with this pain, I thought about how King Saul disobeyed God on several occasions and how God had given him a tormenting spirit (1 Samuel 15). God rejected Saul as king over Israel, "But the spirit of the Lord departed from Saul, and an evil spirit from the Lord troubled him" (1 Samuel 16:14).

Therefore, I went back to King Saul's story in the Bible, and as I read it, I cried the more. In sorrow, I cried unto the Lord daily, asking him to forgive me and to please take me back. I told him that I was deeply sorry and that I don't want to be like Saul. As I sought the Lord in my prayers of repentance, I told him that I didn't want to live any longer in disobedience to him. I repeatedly asked. I pleaded with him to take me back and to take this pain away.

"I don't want to live without you God, and I don't want to live without Jesus," I would cry.

Then, one moment after I had prayed that prayer, a sweet voice also said to me, "King David, a man after my own heart, tried (1 Samuel 13:14). If he could, he would have taken what he did to Uriah the Hittite out of heaven's records" (2 Samuel 12:9).

I, therefore, reread the passage of scriptures and saw truly how David repented before God, found grace with God, and did that sin no more.

Soon after that, over a period of time, God started revealing many things to me through his word. He showed me how Jesus died for my past, present, and future sins; therefore, I should not be committing sins anymore.

Romans 3:23–26 writes: "For all have sinned, and come short of the glory of God; Being justified freely by his grace through the redemption that is in Christ Jesus: Whom God has set forth to be a propitiation through faith in his blood [Jesus's], to declare his righteousness for the remission of sins that are past, through the forbearance of God."

In other words, Jesus's death covers all of the past, present, and future sins of whosoever that believeth in what Jesus has already accomplished on the cross. However, Jesus dying in our place does not give us a license to continue to live in sin or to practice sin willfully (Romans 6:1–4). God has, in the past, tolerated our sins, but now, he's saying no more, because of Jesus. "He has justified us by [our] faith in the finished plan of his to extend salvation to fallen man. We have the gift of a new life in Jesus Christ".

We are sanctified, purified—free from guilt and imperfections—and are cleaned up for God's divine purpose. Based on that, I now understand why God told me that he calls imperfect people for his perfect tasks.

Romans 6:14–16 records: "For sin shall not have dominion over you: for you are not under the law, but under grace. What then? Shall we sin, because we are not under the law, but under grace? God forbid. Know ye not, that to whom ye yield yourselves servants to obey, his servants you are to whom you obey; whether of sin unto death, or of obedience unto righteousness.

Romans 6:23 states, "For the wages of sin is death; but the gift of God is eternal life through Jesus Christ our Lord."

Romans 8:1–2 implies, "God is not condemning us; however, by not believing the word of God regarding Jesus Christ and the cross, we condemn ourselves" (John 3:17-21)

I was one of those Christians who believed that once you accepted Jesus, you could pretty much do whatever you wanted, because that's what Jesus died for (all my sins). However, God showed me in Ezekiel 3:20, that when a righteous man (Christian) turns from his righteousness, and commit iniquity (sin), he shall die in his sin, and his righteousness which he hath done shall not be remembered.

Although we came to God through Jesus as our Lord and Savior, it does not give us, once again, a license to commit or practice sin nor continue to live in our wrong doing; God forbids it, and neither does it give us an automatic place in heaven (Psalms 15:1–5). We are not automatically saved. Jesus reminds us that if we love him, we will keep his commandments (John 14:15), and those who love Jesus will keep his sayings.

In October 1993, I completed a forty-day fast, without food. I drunk only water. In 1994, a year after I completed my fast, my brother, Willie, passed on from this life. I wanted to mention to you beforehand that the details of these years are written herein throughout, as the events of these years and the actual happenings are very important for a better understanding of the writing of this book. God told me in 1995 to write the experience of my dream in a book and tell his people (his churches) that "Hell, It Is Real!" (2 Chronicles 7:14; James 4:10).

I can't, at this time, recall the date but the month could have been July or August 1995. It was summertime. I remember that much, because the school year was in summer session for my kids. One day, just before my children were to arrive from school, I stood near the stove fixing dinner when all of a sudden, I heard, audibly, this sweet, sweet soft voice say, "Tell them." I quickly stopped what I was doing and stood still. I could not move. When I came to myself, I was no longer at the stove, but I was standing right in front of the kitchen sink looking out the window. I realized I was not where I was first standing. What happened? I must have been in a daze.

Thinking about what had just happened, I went to sit down on my staircase, because it seemed as if my life had paused for a moment. Having many thoughts, suddenly, God started to speak to my mind.

"Tell them," and I began to shake my head in disbelief, because these words seem to flow freely. I started to talk back to God and said, "God, is this you? Are you telling me these things?"

As I listened to the sweet voice speaking those words to my innermost being, I later learned that it was Jesus. I had heard this voice many times before, but I had always answered back calling him God; it was Jesus all the time. So I answered him and said, "Lord, my God, how can I go tell them?"

It was like I already knew in my heart what he wanted me to tell and who he wanted me to tell. So I said, "Lord, God, your churches won't believe me. Pastors already don't want women in their pulpits, God."

Then, he said to me, "It's not so much that they believe you, but they will have heard John 15:22 and 1 Samuel 8:6–7. I have opened to you a door that no man can close. Now, go read Revelation 3:7–8."

MY VISION OF HELL

In obedience, I read it:

> And to the angel of the church in Philadelphia write; These things saith he that is holy, he that is true, he that hath the key of David, he that openeth and no man shutteth; and shutteth, and no man openeth. I know thy works: behold, I have set before thee an open door, and no man can shut it; for thou hast a little strength and hast kept my word, and hast not denied my name.

In that moment, my own conviction set in as I began to cry and rejoice at the same time, because I had denied his name and his Word. I lied and sinned before his people openly, but it was as if God had already forgiven me (Romans 8:1–2).

Jesus did not address how I was feeling or my crying; it seemed as though he had a one-track mind: *the message* to the churches. Tell my people and tell my churches, "Hell, It Is Real!" (Psalms 11:6; Isaiah 5:14; Revelations 14:10–11, 20:11–15, 21:8).

Afterward, he (Jesus) told me, "They didn't believe Mary either, but I still rose," reassuring me that everything will be alright (Isaiah 55:8–11).

"It is as if they don't even see I used a woman to give the first sermon of the (my) resurrection. Now, go read Mark 16:9–14."

So, I did.

And it reads: "Now when Jesus was risen early the first day of the week [Sunday], he appeared first to Mary Magdalene, out of whom he had cast seven devils. And she [Mary] went and told them [his disciples] that had been with him [Jesus], as they [his disciples] mourned and wept and they [his disciples], when they [his disciples] had heard [from Mary] that he [Jesus] was alive [had risen from the dead], and had been seen with her [Mary], his disciples believed not."

So, again, Jesus said to me, "It's not so much that they believe you, but they will have heard."

There were so many days and nights I prayed, asking God to help me do what he had asked me to do. I was so worried about what

A SACRIFICE FOR OTHERS TO SEE

people would think, but that didn't seem to worry Jesus at all. He still told me to "Write the dream [the vision] down, put it in a book. Tell my people, tell my churches, that, "Hell, It Is Real!" were his exact words.

Jesus had already let parts of my dream come to pass. I now know it was to spare my soul from being lost. The souls of his people in the churches who say that they belong to him are to wake us all up before it is too late (1 Peter 4:17–19). Although I did not see any faces or recognize any voices but one, God showed me that a lot of individuals, who say they belong to him, will not make it to heaven. I was almost one, and I'm still in a fight daily for my soul.

If you, the reader, as a believer, has ever felt a tug at your heart that makes you draw back and start thinking, then a voice warning you would always come next. That's the Holy Spirit trying to get your attention. That happens every time we are getting ready to do something that's not right, always. Then, consciously, we take a step back, because we begin to realize we are crossing the line in an area that is not morally right in God. If you don't have that tugging, it's because you stopped paying attention to the guidance of God's Holy Spirit and continued doing wrong until you now have become immune to the to the Holy Spirit's leading or conviction. Therefore, your conscience does not bother you anymore, because you have ignored the voice of God for so long until that space of time evolved into years of not listening. Although God has placed in human beings the will to make choices (Deuteronomy 30:19–20 and Luke 4:18–21), we must accept Jesus as our Savior. He's God's choice for man's redemption (Romans 5:12–17). He chasteneth those he loves (Proverbs 3:11–12) when we tend to lean toward the flesh (Hebrews 12:6).

Being so worried about what I was writing, Jesus let me know that what he has shown me is prophetic, true, and will happen, especially since he has shown it to me more than once. Yet there is one part of the dream where I was condemned to that horrible place [to be put in hell's fire]. But God is merciful. He allowed me to realize that if I continue to obey his word, then the latter of my destiny in the dream is that I will not go to hell. I will gain eternal life (John 3:16).

You might be saying to yourself, well that's what he had to do for her. "That is for her," but what has the sweet still voice of Jesus been telling you lately or warning you about? I urge you to listen to that sweet still voice. It could make a difference in your soul's eternal destiny.

Jesus told me that this is how I should know that the dream was real [prophetic]. He gave the scripture in his word that will tell us how we will know if a message [prophecy] or messenger [prophet], or a dream, or vision is true.

Number 1. The order in which I was having the dream each time did not change. It is recorded in the Old Testament (Numbers 12:6). If there is a prophet among you, I the Lord will make myself known unto him in a vision and will speak unto him in a dream.

Job 33:14–15 says, "For God speaketh once, yet twice, yet man perceiveth it not. In a dream, in a vision of the night, when deep sleep falleth upon men, in slumberings upon the bed";…

Since I'm coming to you with a written message, do I claim to have received it from God? *Yes.* Do I claim to be a messenger? *Yes.* A prophet or even a dreamer? *Well, I do not know yet.* That is in God's hand; I am only doing what God has asked me to do. I do, however, believe that God has called me for this particular assignment (Isaiah 58:1).

Am I a servant? Yes, one that has a "made up mind" to accomplish God's will and nothing more. So until he reveals his Divine calling for my life, use me *Lord* (Acts 1:8, John 15:16, and 2 Corinthians 12:1).

Who is the Lord our God? (Psalms 18:30–36, 23:1–6, 24:1–10, 100:3; John 10:30).

1 Timothy 2:4–5 says, "For there is one God, and one mediator between God and men, the man Christ Jesus; Who gave himself a ransom for all, to be testified in due time."

As you read this book, I pray that you will be open-minded and examine yourself by telling yourself the truth. This book is not written to cast condemnation or judgment or to take the place of God's holy word, the Bible. As a people of God, we must keep in mind that in everything we do or don't do, say or don't say we are in every way showing God, every minute of the day, where we want him to put us—heaven or hell.

Writing this book has been the hardest thing for me to do. I've had to tell you just how hardheaded I was (Proverbs 29:1). I did not like to be told what to do. After all, I already knew what to do; I'm an adult, right? Does that sound familiar? In that state of mind, I listened to Jesus partly, not fully, and eventually not at all. I started to listen to another voice (2 Corinthians 11:4). Well not listening to Jesus the Christ, the son of the one true God almost cost me my soul in that dreaded place call "hell." Therefore, God has commanded me to write about it and tell it.

He said to me, "Write it down, Put it in a book, Tell my people, tell my churches, that…HELL…IT IS REAL!"

God has let me know that his people [his churches], the body of Christ, only wants to be entertained and hear what is sometimes called "feel-good sermons." It's as if we are saying, "Tell me anything; just don't talk about my living in sin and/or talk about how I'm on my way to hell, because I *know* I'm going to heaven or God will forgive me. So don't judge me," "God loves me," or "Sing some upbeat songs, not those old slow boring ones."

Well, I thought that God and I had an understanding. I thought that I could serve God, and at the end of the day, I'd be off the clock from representing him. After all, I'm human, so I can do me, my own thing, my way. Well, I found out the hard way that that is devilish and foolishness. I really use to think like that. I would tell myself, "All I have to do is repent, and God will forgive me."

Besides, the power of God just manifested when I sang or prayed. The wisdom of God came forth when I taught Sunday school! However, I was surely found to be so very wrong my friends. I was living daily as a born-again believer, sanctified, and filled with the holy ghost and having the anointing on my life; yet, I did not know I was going to hell from the church! I didn't know I was operating under another spirit, and it surely wasn't the Holy Spirit of God (John 14:15–17 and Romans 8:14).

During my period of repentance, God was letting me know that I was not getting away with what I had done, although forgiven.

He has been uncovering all manner of sin that is being done in his churches from the pulpit to the usher board, to choir members and musicians, and even to the bench warmers, whatever your office may be in the church. For church hoppers, those who are going from church to church and not committing to a ministry, judgment will begin. God has said, "First with us."

1 Peter 4:17–19 writes, "For the time has come that judgment must begin at the house of God: and if it first began at us, what shall the end be of them that obey not the gospel of God. And if the righteous scarcely be saved, where shall the ungodly and the sinner appear? Wherefore let them who suffer according to the will of God commit the keeping of their souls to him in well doing as unto a faithful creator."

As believers, we have confessed to belong to God through Christ Jesus. I'm not trying to scare you. I want all the children of the living God (creator of the heavens and the earth) to be aware that if we are not true to God or ourselves, we cannot be true in the position where we are called to serve him. All sin that God's allowing to be revealed or uncovered will be for all eyes to see as examples of his judgement and must be confessed to God in Jesus name so that that individual's soul can be found not guilty. Sins that are unrevealed or secret sins must also be acknowledged by repentance to God, in Jesus's name, to be found not guilty, or these sins are not forgiven, and the penalty is death (Romans 6:23).

Why does God reveal some sins and not others? It's his judgment, it's his choice (1 Timothy 5:24; Galatians 5:19–21; 1 Corinthians 6:9-11).

Just as parents tell their own children over and over again, "Don't do that" or remind them that bad behaviors have consequences and good behaviors have rewards, God does the same with us as his children. God loves us so much. He does not want to see us go to hell. He really wants us to be in heaven with him. God has called us to live right, and he wants us to live holy before him in everything and in every way absolutely every day (1 Peter 1:13–17; Romans 6:19).

The only way for us to accomplish this is to trust [have faith] in him and his word [Jesus] to work in the members of our body (soul and spirit) daily. Why? Simply because God has said so. In 1 Corinthians 3:16–17, it says, "Know ye not that ye are the temple of God, and that the spirit of God dwells in you? If any man defile the temple of God, him shall God destroy; for the temple of God is Holy, which temple ye are?"

Then, I asked God a question, "Who is considered the righteous, the ungodly, and the sinner?" Then, he answered, "The righteous are the ones who seek my [Jesus] interest" (Matthew 6:33), but seek ye first the kingdom of God and his righteousness, and all these things shall be added unto you. God does not want us to be worried about anything. Just as he takes care of the flowers and birds and they don't worry about when or where their help is coming from, he wants us to have the same faith and confidence, because we know him. He doesn't want us to be faithless. Above all of our needs, wants, or desires, being right in his sight through Jesus is his *FIRST* priority for us (Ephesians 5:27). He wants us to trust in him and seek him in prayer to know his way of doing things. Seek him to know his divine will for our lives. Seek [pray] to be holy for he is holy (1 Peter 1:15–16) and pray to him for a clear understanding of his word (James 1:5–6). Seek him having nothing hidden. Ultimately, lay all that's in your heart before him in prayer. Again, trust and believe that he will always provide what is needed through Jesus and his death on the cross (Philippians 4:19).

Number two. "The ungodly are the ones who do not seek my [Jesus] interests. My [Jesus] kingdom and my [Jesus] righteousness." Jude 1:1–25 tells us how false teachers have crept into the church unaware claiming to be God-sent but are not, disguising themselves as the angels of light. Lacking a true heart in obeying the word of truth preached by our Lord and Savior Jesus Christ. Yet Christ died for the ungodly also. For an ungodly person is also considered one that once walked with God but sinned and whose faith weakened. When warned, they did not turn to God to ask for forgiveness for all unrighteousness is sin (1 John 5:17).

1 John 1:5–10 says, "This is the message: if we confess our sins, he is faithful and just to forgive us our sins, and to cleanse us from all unrighteousness. If we say that we have not sinned, we make him a

liar, and his word is not in us. Such a state can lead individuals into becoming an atheist."

Number three. "The sinner is the one who can't begin to seek my [Jesus] interests, because their hearts are in darkness already, and they cannot see the light of needing Jesus the Savior (Mark 1:15, John 3:15–21, and Acts 2:38).

God's saving grace. For God so loved the world that he gave his only begotten son that whosoever believes in him should not perish but have everlasting life (John 3:16–17).

The character of a dark [evil] heart. And this is the condemnation, that light [Jesus] is come into the world, and men loved darkness rather than light, because their deeds were evil. For everyone who does evil (violation of God's moral principles) hates the light (Jesus), neither cometh to the light [Jesus], lest his deeds [works] should be reproved (John 8:12).

God is looking for doers. But he who does truth comes to the light that his deeds may be manifested, that they are wrought [worked] in God (Ephesians 2:8–10).

God's healing power. John 3:14 says, "And as Moses lifted up the serpent in the wilderness, even so must the son of man be lifted up: That whosoever believeth in him should not perish but have eternal life" (referring to the book of Numbers 21:5–9).

God is our helper. 2 Chronicles 16:9 says, "For the eyes of the Lord run to and fro throughout the whole earth, to show himself strong in the behalf of them whose heart is perfect toward him.";...

Romans 5:8–11 also says, "But God commandeth his love toward us, in that, while we were yet sinners, Christ died for us. Much more then, being now Justified by his blood, we shall be saved from wrath through him. For if, when we were enemies, we were reconciled to God by the death of his Son, much more, being reconciled, we shall be saved by his life. And not only so, but we also Joy in God through our Lord Jesus Christ, by whom we have now received the atonement."

Deuteronomy 30:19 and Romans 6:20–22 says, "So still again we see God in all his love and fairness giving us a choice; death or eternal life."

Seeing with My Eyes, Hearing with my Ears

So now, I realize that every single day, I must stay with God, believing that Jesus took care of everything for me on that cross. I must obey his word. I have found that God has been a revealer and a keeper of his word to me in the vision (Proverbs 20:12;Revelation 21:5–8).

I say that I'm in a fight, but theoretically, we all are, to keep our faith in Jesus and his accomplishments for us (1 Timothy 6:12). We are at war with an enemy we cannot see nor touch, but we can see the effects and the results of his works and what he's capable of (Ephesians 6:12). Our enemy (the Devil, Satan, that old serpent, the great dragon) (Revelation 12:9) is not under our feet; he's using time to make our lives difficult. When we don't keep our minds focused on the things of God, whether by persuasions or by compromising thoughts, Satan's plan is to eventually sift us like wheat, trying to take our souls to hell (Luke 22:31–32). But Jesus have prayed for us to make it.

He's [the Devil] stirring up something daily for each of us, and if we are not watchful and praying (1 Peter 4:7), we will be the ones to fall (Galatians 5:7–8). Ye did run well; "who" did hinder you that you should not obey the truth? This persuasion cometh not of him that calleth you.

1 Peter 5:7–9 says, "Casting all your care upon him; for he careth for you. Be sober be vigilant because your adversary the devil, as a roaring lion, walketh about, seeking whom he may devour; Whom resist steadfast in the faith, knowing that the same afflictions are accomplished in your brethren that are in the world. But the

God of all grace who hath called us unto his eternal glory by Christ Jesus, after that ye have suffered a while, make you perfect, stablish, strengthen, settle you."

As Christians, we can make it (Romans 16:20), if we keep our faith in Jesus [the word], no matter the temptation, no matter the difficulty.

We say *yes* daily to God's word and believe in the finished work of Jesus Christ on the cross, this gives us the power to live a saved life as we walk this fight of faith. When we say *yes* to God's word, we are saying *no* to the Devil. Through Christ, we are more than conquerors (Romans 8:37), if we trust, believe, and obey the word of God. We constantly, in this weak body, need God's help.

Remember, any desire or feeling that keep us in bondage is not of God (Psalms 37:3–8), especially if the need is to go to places or touch those things which are not right for us. Not everything that feels good to us (as a Christian) should be entertained. We must check these feelings out to make sure that they line up with the word of God, because it could be the Devil's leading and not God's (Colossians 2:20–23).

In James 1:12-17, it tells us, "Blessed is the man that endures temptation: for when he is tried, he shall receive the crown of life, which the Lord hath promised to them that love him. Let no man say when he is tempted, I am tempted of God: for God cannot be tempted with evil, neither tempteth he any man; But every man is tempted, when he is drawn away of his own lust, and enticed. Then when lust hath conceived, it bringeth forth sin: and sin, when it is finished, bringeth forth death. Do not err, my beloved brethren. Every good gift and every perfect gift is from above and cometh down from the father of lights, with whom there is no variableness, neither shadow of turning."

God will not give us anything that will cause us to turn from him, his word. Please remember that the gifts God gives to us will cause us to draw closer to him not away from him. God is changing us into a greater image, not like anything of this world's image, but of Jesus, from glory to glory (2 Corinthians 3:18). If anything, we should cry unto him; more of you, Lord, more of you.

A SACRIFICE FOR OTHERS TO SEE

The dream.

The first night I had the dream is where I will begin. My day started as usual like any other day during the week. I went home around 4:00 or 5:00 p.m. after working in the food program at the church. I did my house work and started cooking for the family, while helping my children with their homework. These are the things that I would normally do every weekday anyway. My husband was doing fine, and he too had come home from work and interacted with the family as usual. At this point, I can truly tell you that, from my point of view, everything was just fine. Then, as evening quickly approached, I got the kids bathed and settled down for the night. The kids went to bed before I did. My husband stayed up a bit later as was his norm. When I got into bed, it seems as soon as my head hit the pillow, I fell into a deep sleep and started to dream.

I dreamt that I was standing in a world full of people. As far as I could see, I saw so many people everywhere! I looked from my left, as I turned, it looked like a world full of people. Some standing on various slopes of the mountain tops appeared bigger than others because they were closer. Others appeared much smaller because they were much further away, but still on various mountain slopes in the far distance. The grass all around were golden mixed with white. The skylight was dimmed, bluish grey in color and the sun was not shining. There were people standing around everywhere. I could not recognize anyone's face, nor did I recognize what anyone was saying, except for my brother Willie. As I looked around at all the people, I noticed that everyone, including Willie and I, were dressed in long, off-white garment like gowns. What I still found to be strange was that Willie's voice was the only voice that I could recognize and what he was saying, out of all those people that were there although there were lots of talking going on.

He said to me, "Sheila, I'll be glad, so glad when the trumpet sounds, because when the trumpet sounds. Jesus is going to come back, Jesus is coming back."

He said it with so much excitement, and I replied, "Yes, I know, Willie. I'll be glad too."

Then, everyone around started to rejoice, praising and thanking God as we all stood waiting for Jesus to come back! We knew he was going to come back the same way he left. So we all were looking up to heaven rejoicing saying, "Jesus is coming. Jesus is coming back. Jesus is coming back."

We stood around rejoicing and constantly looking up in the heavens waiting for his return, just like He promised us.

Then, instantly, all eyes shifted and started looking up toward heaven. As we all looked, I, I saw a small dot of light starting to pierce through the clouds in the sky. The dot started out as the size of the point of a sewing needle, just a dot of light. There was utter silence as all eyes were fastened looking up into the sky with great anticipation, because within all of our hearts, we knew what was happening. We all knew that it was Jesus, coming back just like he said he would. The dot of light got bigger and bigger and bigger until the light broke through and filled the whole sky that was once just dim now has become brighter than the sun. Then, it took the shape of a big bright star having five points to it. It lit up the whole sky where we were. Then, everyone stood still. No one moved or said anything. It was totally silent as the big star beamed with such glory. Then, the glory of the star's illumination began to form a shape. The shape became as a man (Numbers 24:17) having one point upward at the top [his head], two points in the middle: one pointing eastward [his right arm] and one pointing westward [his left arm], and two at the bottom pointing downward [his right leg and foot and his left leg and foot]; they were spread apart as in authority, and his feet did not touch the ground.

As soon as I truly realized it was...Jesus...THE TRUMPET SOUNDED (1 Thessalonians 4:16–17). As the trumpet was sounding [this all happened at the same time], my brother Willie went up, and I, I went down. I saw him going up, and I was going down falling, falling, falling. I was going down extremely fast, falling straight down. I wasn't flipping over or fumbling in the air. I was just going straight down, feet first into a dark, dark place (Matthew 8:12, 25:30). I had no control, no stopping, and there was nothing to grab onto to stop me from falling. I was going, going, going straight down. I opened up my eyes once to look around me, but I was going so fast, I quickly closed them because of fear of the speed and the total darkness all around me. I knew then, I was going into hell (Psalms 55:15). I also heard others falling after me as if they were coming down over my head, some falling faster, passing me up falling around my every side. I could hear people [souls] all around me falling into hell screaming hideously saying, "Noooo. Noooooo. Nooooooo. Nooooooo. Noooooooo. Noooooooooo."

Judging from the sound of and in their voices, they too even knew within themselves that, they, like me, had just missed heaven.

As I continued to fall into this place of total darkness, there was no closing off the ears from listening to the cries of the many lost souls. Then, it was just seconds before my feet would hit the ground in hell that this sweet, sweet voice said to me, "It was because your heart [with a pause] wasn't right."

My feet touched the ground, I opened up my eyes, and all I could say was "Oh my God. Oh my God. Oh my God [really fast]. I'm in hell. I'm in hell. Oh my God. I'm in hell."

Over and over again, I repeated those words, because I was not able to say anything else.

(The description of the place has been vividly inscribed in my mind. I've prayed to God that every time I get the privilege to tell it and that every expressed emotion of what I experienced will be manifested as it did when he first took me to hell. It was no longer a dream or vision to me; God actually took me into hell.)

The place I had fallen into was like a room in a cave having rocky walls covered with black substance and not bigger than ten by ten feet. I stood still looking from left to right, trying to find a way out, but there was still none. The place was pitched dark and had a cold, eerie atmosphere. The darkness was so thick and heavy that it pressed against my body. I tried hard to see my way through the darkness, but it was too thick. I could see no light, but what I could see was a white thick, heavy cloudy substance floating in the air. It was almost like fog, but there was no dew or moisture within it; it was dry and cold. I still didn't want to believe that I was in hell, so I still kept just trying to find a way out. I then closed my eyes and told myself, "I'm having a dream, I'm having a dream," but when I opened my eyes and looking around, I realized I was still in the same dark place but couldn't find a way out. Then, as I looked to my right, I caught a glimpse of light within the corner of my right eye. As I continued looking to see where the light could be coming from, a long hallway with a dim light appeared that was not there before.

I got so happy, because I thought I had finally found me a way out, and I knew I was going home. I started to slowly run down this hallway, while holding out my left hand to touch against the rocky wall as a guide, still just trying to get out of that place. I continued to run, now faster toward the middle of the long hallway, realizing that I was almost at the end and the light now getting brighter. Nothing could have prepared me for what I saw next (still yet running with much joy and anticipation of getting out); as I got to the end of that hallway, I turned a sharp corner to my left! Oh my God, I ran into a demon sitting at a desk, and directly behind the demon, was a lake of fire. That was the light that got brighter as I ran down that hallway, it was the lake of fire! I thought the light would get me out of that dark place, but it was actually angry flames blazing some forty feet or so, upward from the lake of fire, high into the air.

Unbelievable fear totally mounted and set in my heart. I knew then for sure that I was in hell. I began to breathe hard, not from running, but from fear and panic. I quickly looked to my right searching for another way out, but still could not find one. There is no way out of here… I said to myself, as that sense of fear and panic continued to grip and overwhelmed me. Then all of a sudden, I saw huge, red, thick flames, shooting up fiercely out of this big opening that looked like the shape of a lake. They were swishing up into the air and down again, one flame after the other, continuously. It reminded me of the waves of an angry ocean hammering up against the rocks of the sea. If you ever heard fire when it's burning something fiercely, then magnify the sound of it one thousand times or more. The sound of it was horrifying.

(God is allowing me to remember everything as it happened the first time, as that is my constant prayer.) And even as I'm writing, I can see everything plainly as if he is introducing it to me all over again. The sounds that I hear throughout the dream [vision], they are indescribable. No human ear can stand to hear such tormenting sounds. Yet I continuously cried, "Oh my God. Oh my God. I'm in hell. I'm in hell. I'm in hell."

I began to look to my left and to my right for another way out, and still found not one. I looked at my right and I saw a long grayish stone table, and on the table was a person [a soul] sitting down screaming in agony for someone to help, but there was no one to help them. The table seemed to be seven or eight feet in length and just about three feet in width. That poor soul was being tortured by these two demons that were standing on the other side of the table. They were laughing together and making fun of the soul on the table, both demons having a deep, hard, evil laugh. They were enjoying themselves so much as they tortured that soul. They didn't know I was standing there looking right at them. I just stood back and watched everything that they were doing. The table had shackles both at the head and at the feet. The two demons then laid the soul down on the table. There was one demon at the head and one demon at the feet of the person [soul]. Then, the demon lifted both arms over the person's [soul] head, placing them into the metal brackets and closing them tightly around the wrist, and then, the demon at the feet did the same with the ankles, locking each one of the ankles into metal brackets and closed them tightly. I could hear weeping, crying, and grinding of the teeth (Luke 13:28). The demon at the head of the table was pointing his long index finger down toward the head of the soul that was on the table, and laughing with an evil laugh….hu hu…hu hu…hu hu…hu hu…hu hu.

As that person [soul] endured that agony, I saw tears rolling down the right side of the face, as I wasn't sure if it was a man or a woman. I'm not sure what the demons did to the table, but somehow, the table started to expand in length, stretching the person [soul] outward (like you would stretch a rubber band). One end pulled the arms, head, and middle of stomach outward to the left, and the other end pulled the waist, legs, ankles, and feet outward to the right. The table was expanding. I could not believe what I was seeing: a person being pulled apart like a rubber band, but the person did not come apart at any of the skin or joints. The body stayed fully intact as it [the soul] screamed out in pain.

I began to break down with tears squeezing, holding, and rubbing my thighs with both hands. I was crying out with such a fear in my heart that I had never known before. *I'm in hell, I'm in hell.* I was looking away trying to see if there was yet another way out, but still there was none.

I then began to hear such a high-pitch scream, and I could feel the torment in the voice as the person [soul] cried out with anguish the words: "Jesus please help meeeeeeeeee."

I grabbed both sides of my face, trying not to hear, and plugging up my ears with my index fingers did not help. I began to cry, saying all over and over again, "Oh my God. Oh my God. Oh my God. I'm in hell. I'm in hell. I'm in hell. I'm in hell."

There was nothing to stop the sound of the crying that tormented this soul. Then the demon at the foot of the table did something to the end of the table to make it click and then the table started retracting back to its original position.

Fear had built up in me more than ever, and I was breathing harder, having realized that I was in a place where there was no hope. I stood there looking at what was happening when out of nowhere that same sweet voice that spoke to me before, (the presence of the voice spoke from the righthand side of me) saying, "I Can't Help Them Now!" Then that sweet voice said… "You would think when they release them the pain would cease, but no my child [with a pause], it hurts the more."

I knew that that voice was no one's but the Lord's. Then his presence was gone from me. I knew that I was standing there alone. I begin to cry the more, saying, "Oh my God. Oh my God. I am in hell. I'm in hell. I'm in hell."

I could not say anything else (Psalms 139:8).

So, I gave in to the fact that I was in hell. I stood there crying, hopelessly, over the thought of never getting out, just crying my eyes out. I didn't know what to do next, since I had already run through the place trying to find a way out and found none. Still crying, I turned to my left, and suddenly, I was back in the first place where the demon was sitting at the desk. The lake filled with flames was still blazing upward on the other side of him just a few feet away (Revelation 19:20 and 20:10 and 15).

The demon got up from his desk and slowly walk forward toward the wall that was made of rocks and having black substance on them. I stood there with my eyes locked on the demon watching his every move. Suddenly, the wall opened up, and out of nowhere, two panels went upward into the wall and two doors appeared. As I stood there waiting to see what would happen next, two tall ugly monstrous-looking demons came walking through those doors. The demons had human like forms, except that they were extremely hideously looking. They appeared to be burnt in their appearance and jet black in color. Their eyes were a large white with a small black pupil in a sunken shape and their teeth were white with heavy gummed and extremely jagged. They had long arm with long pointy finger nails. At first when I looked, it appeared as if they had hoods on, but when I blinked my eyes in fear, I realized that it was the skin that was pleated or gathered together in its natural form, like black charcoal after it has been burnt.

They came forward and stood right next to the demon who was seated at the desk. Approximately five feet in front of me all three demons stood there, side by side. I now began to panic; I was breathing so hard that my chest wall began to raise. If my heart could have come out, it would have as I just stood there wondering what they were going to do next.

All of a sudden, the demon that came over to them from the desk looked at them, and they looked back at him. The two that came through the rocky walls looked at each other. Then, all three looked at me. The two demons that were in front of me lifted up their arms halfway at the elbows having the palms of their hands upwards in front of me and making a beckoning gesture with their fingers as if it was my time to go in that fire (Revelation 20:15).

I fell to my knees crying and screaming, having my eyes clinched tightly. Squeezing my whole body together with my hands and grabbing my clothing tightly into my chest using all the strength within me, I pleaded, saying, "Jeeesus, get me out of this place, please get me out of this place, Lord. I'm sorry. Please get me out of this place. Please forgive me for all my sins. Jesus, I'm sorry. I will tell everybody about hell. I'll tell everybody about this place. I'll tell everybody that hell is real. Jesus, just please get me out, get me out, get me out of this place. Jesus get me out! Jesus get me oooooout!"

Then, all of a sudden, it was as if I was coming up out of a swimming pool full of water. And coming up with my mouth wide open. I took a big, humongous deep breath of fresh air. My eyes popped opened.

My mind started to regulate what had just happened to me; I could think and reason waking up and the knowing part of me woke up. Quickly, I sat straight up in my bed. My face was wet from the tears, mucus running out my nose, and my clothing was soaked with sweat realizing that God had just let me come back from hell (Genesis 2:7; Psalms 30:3, 86:12–13).

When I set up in my bed, I looked over at my husband and saw that he was still asleep. He had slept through it all. I got up to checked on our children; they were still asleep. They never knew what happened. Years passed before my husband knew. His first time ever hearing about my vision was when I told my testimony for the first time at that little church in Watts, California, after my brother, Willie, had already gone home to be with the Lord on May 13, 1994.

Getting in the Fight

Although I was always in constant fear of what could happen to me after I left this life, I did all I could do to show God I wanted to live by his word. My life, my whole frame of mind about him had changed. In October 1993, so determined to show God that I wanted to go to heaven, I did what was [to me] the ultimate fast: forty days with nothing but water, reading my Bible, and staying on my knees in prayer. It felt like I was in hell every single day of that fast, yet I finished it, because I wanted God, and I had to change!

I was "on my knees" praying in my bedroom one evening, and it was as if God cut me off from what I was praying about, and he asked me, "Will you do that even which it takes to break the yokes" (Isaiah 58:6)? God had just given me an open door if I truly wanted to change. I cried and said, "Yes, Lord. Yes, Lord"

I knew in my heart that he wanted me to get in the fight for my soul. By that I mean seeking him in his word, staying before him and constantly wanting to be different. I was lost, like I said, from the church. I knew that he had "humbled" my heart [I gave up to him]. I chose to fast for forty days even though I had already tried once and failed. I knew I couldn't do it alone, so I prayed, prayed, and prayed, *Lord, God, please help me. In the name of Jesus, please help me. I want to be saved. I want to be obedient.*

Then, somehow, God put something in me [a made-up mind] and I began to fast [no doubting, nor questioning him] with water only, no food for forty days. I want you to know this. I know it wasn't just the fasting that helped me, but constantly praying to God in Jesus's name and believing Jesus had already conquered the fast and everything else on the cross. He was with me. Daily, I read my Bible.

It was my spiritual food and strength. Prayer was my lifeline, and I just kept believing (Galatians 5:4–6; Romans 12:1–2).

In short, I suffered greatly in my body. Each day, I felt like I was going through hell, not only experiencing the physical changes that comes from not eating but also the working power that God's Holy Spirit performed delivering me from so many fleshly lustful strongholds that had me bound (Mark 4:19; Titus 2:12; 2 Peter 1:4). Strongholds that I didn't know was in my mind and heart. I was in a war and was almost defeated. The first seven to ten days seemed to be somewhat easy. I would still cook for my family, and being around food was not a problem for me. I continued doing my housework as a wife and mother. I'm telling you that praying, reading the Bible, praying some more, and drinking water was my source of survival for the next thirty days. Things started to change after that tenth day. It seemed like every time after I would pray, something inside me would start to choke me almost to the point that I would almost pass out, and I would have no breath left in me.

Every single day, I would go through this purging. If measured, cups filled with white, some days yellow, and other days, I would throw up clear bitter thick saliva. Some might even say it was from not eating anything. But this would happen to me every other day, during my prayer time, and it continued happening off and on for weeks. During this time of purging, my bodily fluids became uncontrollable as well. I could not make myself stop. I would grab hold of my bed covers or grip the floor carpets and try to cry out for Jesus to help me. It hurt so badly, as if something in knots was holding on pulling my insides out as I would vomit and cough up all this bitter stuff. When it did, I became too weak to move when the Holy Spirit would purge me. I would lay there on my floor in my bedroom, living room, or the bathroom with no strength to move or get up. I never knew when it would happen. I would just lay there and cry out saying, "Lord, please help me," in heavy breaths.

Although it would seem like this process would be hours at a time, but in reality, only fifteen or sometimes thirty minutes would have passed as I would check the time. Afterwards, I would feel lighter, relieved, and very peaceful. I would pray crying out to God saying, "Please help me or I will die doing this fast, but I won't stop my fasting." This is what I would say to God. I had made up my mind [right then and there] that I was ready to die on the fast, and being obedient to God was all worth the suffering. After all, consider how Jesus suffered for my sins (Isaiah 53). The word of God became my food, and prayer truly became my communication line to God the father as I would pray in Jesus's name.

I completed the fast seven months before my brother Willie would go home to be with the Lord. Before that, every time I would see him during that fast, I thought about the dream, the vision. I still didn't tell anyone, no not even Willie. I only talked to God about it, asking him in prayer not to let me go to that dreadful place that God have shown me. Even while I was on my forty-day fast, I was still asking God not to let me go to that place. I know that completing a forty-day fast does not guarantee my place in heaven, certainly not my brother or sister. My salvation is in the finished work of Jesus and what he did on the cross; it's my continued faith. God himself has taught me that truly believing Jesus's death on the cross not only covered all my sins but also covered my fast as well. That's how I was able to complete it. There is nothing we can ever do [works]. The scripture says, "Lest any man should boast." The scriptures say we [every man] are going to be judged according to our works, and my works [that fast] was not going to save me, but the intent of my heart is what God is going to look at in the end. I can't go to hell, I just can't. Hell, it's not an option.

Revelation 20:11–15 says, "And I saw a great white throne, and him that sat on it, from whose face the earth and the heavens fled away; and there was found no room for them. And I saw the dead small and great, stand before God; and the books were opened: and another book was open, which was the book of life: and the dead were judged out of those things which were written in the books, according to their works. And the sea gave up the dead which were in it; and death and hell delivered up the dead which were in them: and they were judged every man according to their works. And death and hell were cast into the take of fire. This is the second death. And whosoever was not found written in the book of life was cast into the lake of fire."

In that, we see that the dead (having no life in Christ Jesus) and those who are not named in the Book of Life will not escape the judgment of God. An individual may deny him now, but I'm telling you… "DON'T DIE without knowing the true way to live" (Isaiah 45:18–25 and Romans 14:8 -12).

God gave me another chance. I often wonder how many people have laid down to sleep only to never awake again in this life. But they entered into eternity now knowing the truth, having rejected Jesus Christ, and not ready to meet the author and finisher of their faith: Christ Jesus and GOD ALMIGHTY (Hebrews 12:2). You see, my friend, a life can come to an end just like that without any warning. We are not gods where we can extend life. Our life is only prolonged by man's support, if God our creator permits. We must be *ready*, believing in our hearts before the time of death (Revelations 22:10–16).

A forty-day fast, I don't advise anyone to do this type of fasting unless, unless, unless God has told you to do so. I tried to do this same fast a few years before, because I had the desire, but I did not make the forty days then. I only made it to day thirty-five with nothing but water. At that time, I stopped, because my body couldn't take the pain for another five days. Truly desiring to please God, even though I completed this second attempt of a forty-day fast, but God did not tell me to do it. However, He did ask me "Will you do what it will take to break the yokes?" (Isaiah 58:4–11).

Because I chose to fast for forty days and prayed for his help the whole way, I believe that he accepted my choice of fasting. Still, however, I don't advise this type of fast for anyone, unless you are directed by God himself.

My Vision of Hell Unfolds by God

After God's dealing with me for so many nights, days, weeks, and months about the vision and my restoration, it was only after Willie's passing in 1994 that God said, "Your dream is no longer a dream but a vision. You have seen you see, I did not let death touch you; I did not leave your soul in hell, but I brought you back. But if you don't straighten up your life, I will put you where I have just shown you. I have called you to the ministry (John 15:16 and Romans 8:28; John 15:16; and Romans 8:28). I will not let you mess up my church. I will kill you first before I let you mess up my church (Proverbs 29:1; Jeremiah 23:1–2; and 2 Corinthians 6:3–10). Straighten up your life for I have called you!"

The memory of this next part would make my heart ache painfully. He said, "Your husband could have awakened to a dead wife, and your children could have awakened to a dead mother, and the coroner could have put on your death certificate, Death Unknown, and I, I could have left your soul in hell."

He continued to say, "Satan has you like a puppet on a string."

Quickly, God showed me a hand [Satan's hand] having pale-colored fingers. The palm of his hand was extended in midair; there was no arm attached. Hanging from each finger were long strings dangling downward, a string hanging from each finger. Having so much sin, sin compounded upon on every string upon each of my fingers. I did not know God had a sense of humor, having taken him so deathly serious throughout the vision and the revelation. I was startled by the next words he spoke. Then, God said to me, "Cut the strings; snip, snip, and tell my people, tell my churches, Hell… It-Is- Real."

MY VISION OF HELL

Suddenly, I came back to myself out of a daze and eager to tell God's people what he had showed me and what he wanted them [his churches] to know. So I began to share my testimony with several pastors who were acquainted with our little church in Watts. Those were the few pastors who allowed me to share my testimony in their churches in Los Angeles.

My friends, I was in hell, and God let me come back. He allowed me to repent of all my sins, whatever they might have been, however many there may have been. I am so grateful he did not leave me in that dreaded place. I knew that I did not want to be that sinful person anymore.

Many days later, I asked Jesus, "Lord, why do you love me so much? Why are you so merciful to me after all I've done?"

Then, he answered in such a sweet, sweet voice as if he used his index finger and tapping each of these words into my heart, each word one by one and said, "For...my...love...has...covered...your...multitude...of sins" (1 Peter 4:8).

I fell to my knees on the floor of my living room. It was as if all strength and almost life itself had left my body, helplessly overwhelmed by God's touch.

I stayed on my knees crying out to the Lord, asking him to help me. *Don't let me go; please don't leave me.*

It was then, and only then, that I knew in my heart the true love God the father and Jesus had for me. It was the love I should have already known.

This love God has, he said, "It's not for me only, but it is for all who dare to have faith to believe to the point of keeping his every word. 'Jesus' is the word of God as is declared throughout the whole Bible" (John 1:1–18).

Why, because of God's salvation Plan for mankind? As believers, we need both the Old and New Testaments to completely understand God's great reconciliation plan through his son Jesus Christ. (2 Corinthians 5:19 and Isaiah 53:1-12)

Out of fear, I had no choice but to tell someone about my vision. My brother, Willie, who was in my vision had just passed away from diabetes, a disease that was never diagnosed. He never took a drop of insulin in his thirty-three years of life, because he didn't like going to doctors. As a result, he never knew he had the disease. Several weeks earlier, he had become sick with flu-like symptoms, for which he took regular over-the-counter medications trying to get better, but he didn't. Not only was Willie the assistant pastor of our church, but he was also one of the overseers in the food ministry.

The morning of his death, he went on a food pickup for our seniors' Brown Bag Program. My other brother, John, also knew that Willie was not feeling well. He called him earlier that morning to tell him that he would do the food run so that Willie could get some rest. However, being the kind of person that Willie was, he had already left for the pickup, driving a twenty-four-foot bobtail truck. I arrived at the church office later that morning. Being that I was the office manager, everyone started to ask me about the food pickup since Willie was late getting back. In addition, we also had seniors already standing in line that day for the Brown Bag Program. Everyone thought it was unusual that the food had not yet been delivered. All of a sudden, someone yelled, "Look at the truck. Willie can't stop the truck!"

The truck was swerving back and forth, and food is dropping off the truck! We all ran out of the office to see what was going on. My brother John ran as fast as he could down a two-lane busy street (at 103rd and Grape streets) and jumped inside the truck to stop it. Willie had no more strength, he was very weak. As we looked down the street, there was a trail of food boxes that had fallen from the truck. The people in the neighborhood were kind enough to bring them back to the church. John made sure Willie made it home safely. We didn't wait. We took him to the hospital right away. The program for the seniors went on as scheduled. John, Bonnie, Willie's wife, and I took Willie to the hospital where the doctors ran all kinds of tests on him. John had me call our mom in Arkansas to let her know what had happened.

I called and told her, "Madear, Willie has become sick, and the doctors need to know if we have any diseases that run in our family that they need to look out for specifically."

She said, "Baby, have the doctors to check for diabetes. It runs in our family."

Sure enough, that's what it was. The doctors said that they couldn't understand it. He should have already been dead or in a diabetic coma. His sugar level was up in the 1000 ths. The doctor asked us how long had he been sick. All of us had the same answer: for about two weeks with flu-like symptoms. So they started giving him the insulin, and a few hours afterward, his vital organs started to shut down. His kidneys went first. All the other organs shut down soon after.

This all happened on the same day when he'd make sure the seniors got fed. Willie went home to be with the Lord. He was "faithful" to the work of the ministry until his passing. This is what God requires from all those who are believers (Revelation 2:10).

When that part of what God had showed me actually became true, I finally had to tell my pastor what God had showed me twice in 1992. Willie was really gone, and now, a part of my dream had actually come to pass!

My pastor asked me, "Sheila, why you didn't come to me? We could have prayed to ask God to reveal your dream."

I told him it was because I was ashamed, and now, the dream was starting to form right before my eyes.

Because of my dishonesty, God did not lead neither my pastor nor the first lady to pray for me, but I know they were praying for me in their private closet to the Lord without them saying. So, from that time on and from time to time, they would let me tell the dream to the congregation in our little church in Watts. This was even the beginning of my husband hearing my testimony. And, oh, how the Holy Spirit would just move on hearts in the service, and many who were not saved became saved, and those who were saved came to the alter also before the Lord examining their lives.

I thank God that he showed me so much of his love and mercy in my struggles to write. It was difficult to do. God didn't stop talking to me. He did not let me die in my many sins, nor did he let me keep on sinning without a warning. God could have allowed me to receive a reprobate mind (Roman 1:28 and 2 Timothy 3:8), not worthy of heaven, and believe the lie "once saved is always saved" as the truth because I did turn from his word and backslid. Then, I lied.

God warns us through the scriptures that when a righteous man turns from his righteousness and commit iniquity, then his righteousness which he hath done shall not be remembered. Nevertheless, if thou warn the righteous that thou sin not and he doeth not sin, he shall surely live, because he is warned…. (Ezekiel 3:20-21). I recall, months after my brother's passing in 1994, that I prayed fervently again to the Lord one night, because there were many moments of uncertainty in my Christian life even after my fasting. Some days, I felt the warm presence of Jesus with me, and some days, it was as if I was walking alone (those were the days I did not feel his presence with me). That loneliness occurred many times. I thought to myself, *Willie is gone. I can't talk to him.*

My other brother John would come talk to me. I was happy about that. Bonnie, his wife, would make herself available, but I still felt alone in my heart. I had no joy. I prayed and asked God to send me a sign that he's still with me.

I prayed, "God, please, I don't want to be lost."

It didn't happen that night or the next week, but months later, I fell into another dream separate from the first dream God gave me. My brothers and sisters, I know many of you will be troubled with me asking God for a sign, but I ask you to please keep reading to hear what he says.

I dreamed that I was standing outside the door of the church's community outreach office. I was looking out at the parking lot where we always had many pallets of food set up. On this particular day, the yard was cleaned as if all the food had been put away in the storage shed that was built on the premises. The full length of the grounds still had a chain-link fence around the perimeters, and the parking lot was spotless. There were no cars parked in the lot nor on the side street adjacent the church. As far as I could see, there was no one else at church but me. As I continued gazing out into the parking lot, all of a sudden, I began to hear whistling and dangling of keys. I stood still just outside the office door, looking to see where the sounds were coming from. There was a little blind spot at the new

MY VISION OF HELL

entry door in front of the church, so I had to stretch out my neck and leaned toward my left shoulder to see who it was. My first thought was that it was the pastor because he used to swing his keys making the same sound.

Looking further, I saw that it was Willie coming out of the church door. He turned right heading toward the chain-link fence and began to walk parallel to the fence from one corner of the church property to the other side where I was standing. It was as if he was doing a security check, making sure everything was okay. I continued to stand there looking at him, because I was saying in my mind, *Wait a minute. Willie is in heaven; this can't be him.*

He continued walking the length of the fence looking down at the ground, whistling and swinging his keys, which he would do from time to time when he was still here with us.

Although my eyes were fixed on him the whole time, he did not see me until he came around the corner of the storage building toward the office. He looked at me, and I looked at him. Willie was dressed in the same dark-green overalls that he used to wear while working, and he had on the same thick brown leather back brace and a type of baseball cap that he would always wear when working.

So he came over to me and stood right in front of me and asked, "What's wrong, is everything okay?"

Without hesitation, I said, "No one will have anything to do with me. No one will talk to me. I don't even know if God loves me."

He put his hand out toward me as if to stop me before I could say anything else. As I stopped talking, he said, "Sheila, God loves you, and no matter what anyone else says, you just stay faithful."

He turned and walked away as he repeated, "Just stay faithful. God loves you. Just stay faithful."

He went back into the church. I woke up full of hope.

There have been countless hurdles to conquer. I've had some failures in making the jump. With God, I have found that clearing the jump with the hurdle still standing is always possible. This is still my goal. The hopeful feeling was not always strong within me, but hope never left. God is greater than all my hurdles. I know that I am a conqueror through Christ Jesus who strengthens me through his spirit (Romans 8:37). I thank God for allowing Willie to visit me with such a message, reminding me to stay faithful and that God loves me. God is with me in my many struggles with life and its circumstances. I even struggled with asking God for a sign (1 Samuel 28:5–20; Matthew 12:38–45; Mark 8:11–12). I prayed and said to God, "I believe in you, and I wasn't questioning the deity of Jesus or asking foolish questions. I can only be saved by you [Jesus] helping me. I was feeling so bad. I needed to know if you heard my every prayer saying, 'Help me Lord. Help me,' because I needed a miracle from *you*, Lord."

Finally, days later, God lead me to Isaiah 7:10–14 where God granted King Ahaz a moment for him to ask for a sign, a miracle. It was just moments after reading the scripture that my heart was at peace.

I believe in my heart that because I went to God with a right heart, in faith, and for myself asking for a sign, he granted it. I didn't ask my pastors to agree in prayer with me, and we should (Matthew 16:19 and 18:19). I went to God in prayer, and really, I had forgotten about it. As a believer in the one true God our creator and his son Jesus the Christ, any other way of seeking an answer from God other than his word according to the scriptures is a form of witchcraft. We must make God's word the final authority in our lives (Leviticus 19:26, 31, 20:6, 27; Acts 16:16–19)

Even after Willie came to me in that dream, God still let the vision unfold right before my eyes, and He said to me, "It's "The Vision," a sacrifice for others to see." I let you come back to tell my churches (tell my people) that…Hell…It…Is…Real.

My Prayer and My Song

When God told me that, I made several requests to him in prayers, asking:

> God, in the name of your holy son Jesus Christ, my Savior, in whom I put all my trust, please help me to pen this book. Please give an ear to my prayer. I want this writing to be anointed, that hearts and minds will be captivated by every word that is written. This is your testimony Lord, and I am just your witness. (Matthew 7:7–8 and (James 1:5–6)."
>
> As I continued, I said, "Lord, and after this book has been published and in the hands of many or on store shelves with some fumbling over it, moving it trying to get to another book, or even looking at the cover just to read the title that, by your Holy Spirit, this book will be chosen by them, taken home with them, and completely read. Please give the reader the understanding that you are truly real in every word that's written within these pages.
>
> May you, father God, get all the glory and your holy son Jesus in whom I put all my trust. Thank you, father God for giving me another chance to get it right with you. In Jesus's name, I pray. Amen.

You see, my heart has even longed for God's message in this book to be published throughout all nations that souls might be saved, and God's own people will truly believe and understand the truths that he has given me to tell. It has not taken God all this time to give me this message; it took me all this time to be obedient to him.

I've asked God that in every opportunity he gives me to tell my testimony of hell in person, that He allows me to experience the same intense moments as if it's the first time He let me fall into the vision, and to let it come forth with His Holy Anointing power that saves. And if He would let me hear the same tormenting sounds, and that I could make the same sounds I hear with my natural mouth.

Even with the sound of the trumpet, I have been asking God, "Lord, what about the sound of the trumpet?"

I knew it was blowing, but I could not hear it. Why couldn't I hear it? I would like to express that sound. And his sweet voice said, "It was because your heart wasn't right" (Psalms 78:31–39). And not within a minute, the scripture that came quickly to my mind was, "My sheep knows my voice." I quickly had to find it and read it along with all the other scriptures he brought to my mind (John 10:1–4; John 18:37; 1 Corinthians 15:52, 1 Thessalonians 4:16; Revelation 1:10).

As I read the passages over and over again, I then understood why I did not hear the sound of the trumpet, it was as Jesus said, "My heart wasn't right" (John 5:24–25). Only the saved will know Jesus's voice, and only the saved will be able to hear the sound of the trumpet. I thought I was saved, but I was unsaved in my heart. I didn't fully give my whole heart to God. I gave him only the parts I wanted him to have. I wasn't being true to God, giving him only half of me. While all of me is what he wants, all of me truly need his help (Colossians 1).

I pray for his continued strength as I go forth telling about this vision. God has already told me this, "It's not so much that they believe you, but they will have heard."

That statement reminds me of Jesus in John 14:8–11, when Philip wanted to see God, and it would satisfy him, but Jesus told Philip, "Listen, Philip. Believe me that I am in the father, and the father is in me or else believe me for the very works' sake."

MY VISION OF HELL

In other words, "Sheila, this is going to be hard for you to do and hard for many to receive. They don't have to know you; they don't even have to believe that you are mine. Just do as I have told you. Write it down. Put it in a book. and I'll do the rest" (John 15:22).

Again, my friends, everything in this book has been revealed to me by God's tender mercy, bringing me out from being disobedient into his saving grace. So my prayer is that I am led in the fullness of God's spirit, always. The years of my life have been full. I've been down many roads of troubles and trials, and I'm sure it's not over yet. But the good thing about that is I'm trusting in Jesus to keep me and bring me out of them all.

Romans 8:28 says, "And we know that all things work together for good to them who love God, to them who are the called according to his purpose."

It was in 2000 when God gave my son beautiful music on the piano to a song. He was so discouraged, because he couldn't come up with any words for the music. So I told him, "Let's go to the book of Psalms. Let's pray and ask God to give us the words."

Well, when I turned my Bible, the page fell on Psalms 88. I immediately just started singing the first verse and then the second verse, and the words fit perfectly. When we got so far into more verses, God then led me to Psalms 86 showing me verses which fit perfectly to end the song. I began to realize that in all my years of praying to God, these are the words I had been saying to him along the way. It was in reading Psalms 88:2 over and over again that the title came to me. "Give an Ear to My Prayer."

I would pray for our children all the time, but it came to a point when it seemed I had to pray even more for them. I have sung "Give an Ear to My Prayer" down through the years. It's my anthem. I need God to hear me. I have had many troubles, trials, and even struggles while writing this book. It was in 2001 when all seemed to go downhill; there were so many distractions. My husband and I endured situations regarding our children that would have many people, I believe, simply give up on God. I used to run after our children to find them at their friend's houses. All of these pursuits to save my own flesh and blood seemed to be doing more harm than good. This only intensified my own anxieties, stresses, and strains. I saw myself giving up on life.

Unexpectedly, one night in prayer, God asked me a question, "Why are you killing yourself? They are not listening to you. They are not listening to me. So why are you killing yourself? If you die from worry, they will still not listen to me. So why are you killing yourself?"

Those words snapped me back into reality. Finally, I stopped running after them, and I prayed and turned my children over to God, especially the four oldest of the seven. Then, my prayer became, "Lord, please save all of my children. Put people in their paths they will listen to who have your words in their mouths." Then, just as God had told me, I, one day, told my husband. I, I apologized for the frustrations I caused for not listening to him. Days after that with my husband, their father, I spoke to all our kids and told them also what God had said to me, and I was not going to kill myself with worrying or running after them anymore. I had asked God to take care of them. From that moment, I felt free. I continued to pray, because no matter how far my children may stray, he will bring them back. He will save them all. That's his promise (Proverbs 22:6).

I give him all the honor and glory for his loving kindness and tender mercies that has been bestowed upon me. Also, I must tell you that through my many deep hard failures, troubles, trials, and tears, I am learning to be obedient to God by living his word [whatever Jesus has said], and I have made it to be the final authority in my life and to respect the Holy Spirit. It convicts me when heading in the wrong direction and comforts me when I am going right. Thank God he's the spirit of truth.

Jesus has paid the highest price so I [whosoever will] can make it. As a result, he guarantees our life will be changed if we believe and stay with his word and continue to seek God for our personal walk in him. It's a mystery in God's wisdom just how a person can change to live for him in this life free from sin and change to live saved for the life to come. I thank God for offering up Jesus on that cross, it's his work of salvation (John 12:32, 1 Corinthians 2:7-8)

MY VISION OF HELL

My friends, I thought I was already saved, sanctified, and filled with the holy ghost, speaking in tongues, and on my way to Heaven, as I've said before. Then, God gave me a rude awakening one day, and I realized that I wasn't going to heaven. I wasn't going to make it unless I made a change. I needed help with the many lustful desires working in my mind, my heart, and then eventually in my flesh [my body]. If the enemy can get to our mind, then the heart and body will follow (Romans 12:1–2).

Jesus said to me that *my heart* wasn't right, as I was entering hell. When I woke up from that dream, that's when I saw myself hell bound for the first time, as a Christian from the church. Whatever my position was in the church, it did not matter to God. What mattered was my actions did not reflect my faith nor was it representing him or his word [Jesus]. Like Eve, I was deceived, my mind got off the word, and then I lost my faith. I fell into unbelief and, today, so have many of God's people in his churches (2 Chronicles 7:14; Psalms 78:34–39; 2 Corinthians 11:3–4).

A SACRIFICE FOR OTHERS TO SEE

My Song: Give an Ear to My Prayer
Taken from: Psalms 86 and 88
Written by: Shelia M. Drummer and Michael C. Drummer II
Year: 2000

O Lord God of my salvation, I cry day and night before thee
I lift my heart up before thee, for I am poor, and I am needy
Preserve my soul, make me whole, save thy servant for I trust in thee
O Lord I want to walk in thy truth, unite my heart to fear thy holy name
Jesus turn to me, for great is thy mercy, and give an ear to my prayer
Lord, I need you to hear me, give an ear to my prayer.
Among the gods there is none like thee, for all the nations shall worship thee
For thou are great, and thou are strong, and thou my Lord,
Well you are God alone
Preserve my soul, make me whole, save thy servant for I trust in thee
For my soul rejoice, in thee 0 Lord, and now, well I lift up my soul
O Lord I want to walk in thy truth, unite my heart to fear thy Holy name Jesus
Turn to me for great is thy mercy, and give an ear to my prayer
Lord I need you to hear me, give an ear to my prayer
When I'm on my knees praying, wash me, heal me, Lord Jesus sanctify me
I need you to give an ear, Lord Jesus, I need you to send me an answer,
Send me an answer, I need an answer. Lord Jesus…
Give an ear to my prayer.

Innocence Taken, But God

For twenty years, I had struggled with promiscuity. It was at the age of being fifty years old when I would pray and ask God why those things had to happen to me as an innocent little girl. These things caused me to be in such a battle. I didn't blame him, but I felt like I would have been a different person if I had not been taken advantage of as a child. I told Jesus as I prayed to him crying, "Jesus, I was six years old when I accepted you into my heart at our family's church. I remembered that I wanted and tried to be good and to do what Madear and Daddy asked of me. Then, I lost it [crying as I continued in prayer]; I didn't have that feeling for you anymore after I started being molested."

Then, Jesus's reply to me was, "Yes, many hands has touched you. At a baby's age, Satan's plan was to destroy you. But that wasn't my plan. What happened to you wasn't my will, but look at you now, my child. Look at you now. Look at you now. Look at you now."

His voice fading out as he was saying, "Look at you now."

Then, I cried even more, because all I still saw were my failures down through those years. Yet he said it wasn't his plan (Jeremiah 29:11).

As I continued in prayer, Jesus allowed me to experience his overwhelming presence and showed me the father's mercy in my life down through those same years of my failures. I now know it was God tugging at my heart to do what was right. My life could have been cut short. But he was the one making ways for me to come out of my darkness and into his marvelous light (1 Peter 2:9-10). At this point, his love overwhelmed my heart, as he still does for me so many times today. During these times, all I can do is just praise him, and

I begin to speak in another tongue as his Holy Spirit gives me the utterance (Acts 2:1–4; Romans 8:26–27).

From the age of six to the age of fourteen, I was molested by family members both male and female and by some of my siblings' friends. I was so confused as a child and broken in spirit growing up. After the abuse would happen, the individuals would always tell me, "If you tell anyone, no one will believe you."

As a little child, I believed those lies all along until I finally fought back. I kept all these happenings locked up inside of me all those years while living a lonely life of fear, although I was surrounded by my family members. As the eleventh child of a share cropper's family, chopping and picking cotton was our only source of income. Our father and mother not only taught us that we must love each other as kids but also that a family must work together to be successful. There were five boys and eight girls. In addition, our parents raised our father's niece, which brought the number to fourteen children all growing up in our home. We were at church every time the doors where open. Our father made sure that we went to church. As a matter of fact, he added a rule: We all had to get our church clothes ready by Wednesday or Thursday, because getting them together on Sunday morning would cause the family to be late. I truly love my family, and I wouldn't trade them for the world. I'm glad I had a mother and father who taught us family values and loved us dearly, teaching us not to fight and argue among ourselves. More importantly, Daddy kept God's word before us and would tell us always that "a disobedient child's days shall be shortened." Even in all the good, there was a secret, a secret that almost destroyed me.

Then, in 1977, at the age of fourteen, I finally got the courage to speak out to one individual who molested me more than the others. I was asleep in my bed one night, and it was as if someone was having sex with me, and I didn't want to in the dream. I dreamed that I was fighting the person off of me. So, I quickly woke up in the natural. When I opened my eyes, the person was really on top of me. I looked straight in his eyes and said, "if you don't get off me, I will scream out so loud, and I don't care who hears me, who will or will not believe me, but you will not do this to me ever again!"

He began to beg me, "No, no, don't tell on me. I'm sorry. Sorry, I won't do it again."

I still didn't tell anyone else, but that individual never touched me again. After that night, no one every molested me again! I saw in that action [literally opening up my mouth to stand up for myself] that I had empowered myself. Although too late, it seemed on my part, but I did not want to be hurt again.

So at fourteen years of age, I prayed days later and asked God, "Please, let Madear and Daddy say we can go to California. Please God."

As time passed, I had forgotten about that prayer. You see, before I had prayed, two of our older sisters had previously asked if our baby sister and me could come live with them in California. Well, Madear said, "No."

So, we couldn't go to California. Of course, I said to myself, "Sheila, why didn't you speak out before?" (I just didn't know that I was going to get this result.)

I started feeling okay. Those years are going to be behind me now, but regrettably, I felt that I couldn't do anything about them. Then, a few years later, in July of 1979, Madear said, "Yes."

Shortly afterward, my little sister and I were on that Greyhound bus headed to California.

I was sixteen years old. I knew this would be the turning point to a happy life. I knew no one would touch me again. I felt free of that. I was on top of the world, especially after meeting this tall, dark, and handsome young man next door who was two years older. As it turned out, he would become my husband a few years later. The day we arrived, he carried my luggage inside my sister's house which was next door to his house. At least, I thought I was on top of the world in a new state, a new city, and with new friends. Unfortunately, this is where I also started making more bad choices as a teenager that lasted for more than twenty years.

I never regretted becoming a mother and wife at the age of eighteen. I was determined to graduate from high school; and I did. It was inwardly; it seemed as if I was torn, confused, and trying to process past hurts while wanting to be a good wife and mother looking at the wonderful example from my mom.

A SACRIFICE FOR OTHERS TO SEE

In the early years of my marriage, intimacy with my husband was hard, because I would have flashbacks, even nightmares, of someone molesting me. I would want to run with my friends to parties and concerts and forget that I was a wife and mother.

And, oh, how I've had to ask my husband for his forgiveness. His reply to me was, "Sheila, I love you. I know that it wasn't you."

However, it was only one month after we started dating that, in confidence, I told my husband what was done to me as a child. He lovingly held me in his arms and has never made mention of it (or used it in any negative way] these thirty-nine years of being in each other's lives. God also showed me that my husband's heart is very tender. By this, I mean that although the contents of this book represent my personal testimony, I could only say what God would allow. From my heart, I gave credit to the way I was and that my behaviors were the result of what happened to me as a child. That being the human side of us and what we normally do to protect ourselves by putting the blame on someone else. Now, I know it was wrong to do that.

This blame game has been going on since the days of Adam and Eve in the Garden of Eden (Genesis 3:12–13). And the man said, "The woman whom thou gavest to be with me, she gave me of the tree, and I did eat."…And the woman said, "The serpent beguiled me, and I did eat."

Growing up, many times, I wanted to tell my parents about what was happening to me, but I thought that they wouldn't believe me, because by the age of nine or ten, I had become an angry and rebellious little girl. I ran away from home one time, and because of my many negative actions, I felt they would not have believed me. That was something planted even in my mind by those who would molest me. All those years, while feeling alone, there was a pull in my heart to do right. But I would always choose to do the opposite. Oh, how I thank God always for his mercy.

In 2009, I reached out to one of my sisters, and as I shared with her what was done to me as a child, I didn't realize that this abuse still had such a grip on to my heart, even after talking to Jesus about it. I still felt like something was taken away from me, and that I would never find out what type of person I could have become instead of the person I lived as; having endured all those years of childhood molestation. She was in tears with me and said, Sis, you are not alone."

Although she did not say it, and I did not ask, but from what she said, I believe in my heart that it had happened to her as well. From that day until now, we have never mentioned it again, and we have seen each other three times; in 2011, 2013 and 2017 at our family gatherings. Since then, I've just prayed and asked God to mend my heart from the scars that the abuses have made and left; because of the residue, I was still feeling there were also still lots of triggers. And I want to be blessed and be a blessing to his people in ministry.

It was in 2014 when I was working on the book with Pastor Bonnie, and straightforward as always, she asked me, "Pastor Sheila, have you told your family you are writing this book?"

I replied, "No, ma'am."

She began to say, "You cannot move forward with this book until you have spoken to each of your family members. What if they read this, and they don't know what has happened to you?

I tell you a fear set in my heart. I started to think, *They just won't believe me.*

Then, I had to regroup my thoughts, because I realized that those words were a trigger. They took me back to a place that reminded me of what was told me as a little girl, "No one will believe you." It took a few days, and I prayed each day, asking God to give me the strength I needed to call everyone, even my mother. Today, I look at my life and see that God's true peace did not come until I phoned my siblings and our mother to share the secret I had been keeping for all these years. Obviously, it's no longer a secret. I made the calls. I cried, and they all cried with me.

God used several of my siblings' responses to confirm some of the very same things that Jesus had said to me through the journey of writing this book. One of my sisters said, "Glory be to God, Sheila. Look at you now."

Another sister told me, "The enemy tried to destroy you, but God had you all along."

A SACRIFICE FOR OTHERS TO SEE

The tears continued to flow as I retold the story each time. However, God allowed me to hear and feel the love and compassion that was instilled in us by our parents.

Ultimately, the most difficult call would be to our mother. My sisters, who are my mother's caregivers, (had me on speaker phone) said to me, "Sister, Mother [Madear] has to know; you must tell her."

I cried, "No, I don't want to hurt Mother. She's aged eighty-six years old."

After much debate and a quiet moment, I agreed to call Mother. I told my sisters to just give me a minute and to let me call her right back. They both agreed. It was less than five minutes. I wanted to get it over with. I made the call. At first, even though I hesitated and felt ashamed, I fumbled for words, but I finally got it all out. I did it. I told her all about how I had been molested from the age of six to fourteen years old. I was weeping uncontrollably when my mom said to me, "Baby, me and Daddy didn't know. We would have done something, Baby. We would have. Momma is sorry. Please forgive me."

At this point, the tears began to flow even more. Then, she said, "Don't cry anymore, Baby. You don't have to hurt anymore."

When my mother said that, even though we were thousands of miles apart, I felt like that innocent little girl again. My heart and soul were comforted by my mom's words, words that seemed to embrace me as if I was in her arms. Still, I cried.

Then, my chest felt as light as a feather. I held my chest and cried more. My tears were transformed from shame into joy and deliverance. I started to feel as if a weight had been lifted off of my chest, and I could not stop crying for the joy and peace that was beginning to fill my heart (John 14:27).

Our father went home to be with the Lord in March of 1992. It was after his death that I started to have [the] dreams of the vision of hell. I am proud to say that our dad is with Jesus. The lifestyle our father built as a family was a legacy. It was a legacy of love and service to God, love and protection for the family, hard work, and dependability. We are a close family. If I had told my parents that their son, my brother, had been molesting me (for years), I believe there would have been a tragedy in our home. It would have torn our family to pieces. My father would have hurt my brother, or, even worse, killed him. You might think that I am strange, but I am glad that I did not say anything. I believe it was God who held my mouth through the pain. I understand everyone has something in life to go through (Colossians 1:23–29; Romans 8:17–18), and I am glad that my life is "the sacrifice for others to see." Although it was a horrible journey for me, I now realize that God was working all the time.

Despite the pain and shame I have felt through the years, I would not trade my testimony, since I now know the faithfulness of God. My family is not torn apart but saved in Jesus's name. My mother and many of my siblings are active servants in God's ministry. Glory be to God.

Once again, the evil that was against me, God made it good. Glory be to God. Look at me now. Look at my family now, stronger than ever in the love of God almighty. My siblings and I stand together with our mother to pass on our father's and her legacy to the third, fourth, and possibly the fifth generations of our family and to also be witnesses to others that Jesus Christ is real and is Lord.

I look at my life as a living testimony of God's grace and mercy through Jesus Christ and what he did on the cross. I have long, long ago forgiven those individuals, and I pray for their salvation always or at least for those who maybe still alive. I don't hold any grudges against them. And regarding my failures, I have forgiven myself. And if I even think I might have done something (not willfully) out of the will of God, I'm repenting sorrowfully and genuinely out of so much reverence and love I now have for God (John 14:15). I don't take my walk with God lightly. I don't ever want to get comfortable, because I want to forever in my heart have Jesus's warmth and *peace* and *joy*.

I know he's with me, and I'm no longer ashamed, because God, in Jesus's name, has forgiven me. He has set me free from all those strongholds that had me bound. With God's help through his son Jesus and his precious Holy Spirit, I've been standing strong since 1997. By God's grace, I will live in him until he comes back for me. I will continue telling my vision of hell and God's dealings with me and him restoring me back into his favor. You see, we all can make it with God's help if we just dare to believe that we are forgiven, sanctified, cleaned up, and made anew by the precious blood of the only begotten son of God, our Lord and Savior Jesus Christ (John 8:36).

If you, the reader, are going through anything, and you are seeking God's redemption, he has made it so simple; just repent and believe. God has provided through Jesus' death on the cross forgiveness of all of our sins, deliverance, healing, and above all, love. If he did it for me, he will certainly do it for you, if you should ask; as he is no respect of persons. God see all of us the same, needing a Savior. Always remember the great invitation, and the more abundant life which God has given us through his son Jesus Christ. (Matthew 11:28-30 and John 10:10)

This is what helped me to understand and believe that God will accept you as you are as a sinner, BUT he truly desires that we accept his great salvation plan for man. And where sin is, God has shown in the scriptures his presence is not. There is eventually a separation (Genesis 3), as it is written in Genesis 3:22-24, God provided us a remedy (Romans 5:12-21).

According to John 3:3-21, Jesus himself, told a ruler of the Jews (Nicodemus), that he must be born again. That is Jesus's message to everyone, who want to go to heaven; because remember, that Hell, It…Is…Real! Jesus has paid the way and has shown us how to get there. Having said that, we have to be careful even how we come to church to worship the Lord. For we know that the church is not just a constructed building, but the church is the Bride of Christ! (Revelations 21:9)

The Closing

It was sometime in 2008 when I started praying fervently saying, "Please, God, give me the understanding of the cross and Jesus's death on that cross."

And genuinely, that's how I said it. I was hungry for more of God. Over the years, I have had to change my life to comply with his *word*. It was hard to change; I had to get away from lying to God, others, and myself. I thought that I was okay the way I was when, truly, I was a miserable person while serving in the ministry. Then, God himself had to reveal to me that there are so many false things that have been planted in the church, in the body of Christ, and so many of his people are falling for them all., and I was one.

It was on Christmas Day, December 25, 2008, when Pastor John and Bonnie gave me a gift. When I opened the gift, it was the *Expositor's Study Bible* by Jimmy Swaggart. As I glanced at it, I soon remember how my father and mother with all the kids would sit around in our living room and watch the Billy Graham and Jimmy Swaggart crusades on television; that had to have been around the '70s or early '80s. So I just placed the Bible on the head of my bed and left it there. Months had passed, and I was in my bedroom looking for another Bible to carry, because I had read my old Bible so much until many of the pages had come loose, and I had already started using tape to keep them together. That's when I saw the *Expositor's Study Bible* that I had received and placed on the headboard of my bed. I took it down and held it, and I began to remember the Jimmy Swaggart Ministry, and I thought to myself, *and now he has a Bible out?*

Anyhow, it was days after that, as I was scrolling up my cable channel to find a gospel station, I ran into Jimmy Swaggart, and ironically, he was preaching hard on the message of the cross! I still didn't use his study bible at the time, because it was hard for me to give up my old one. So, I started to watch Jimmy Swaggart's programs off and on, but not faithfully. Then, it was in 2009, I can't remember the exact day, I was watching Jimmy Swaggart again on one of my cable channel 344, and again, he was preaching on the message of the cross, but it had not dawn on me what God was doing. However, as Jimmy Swaggart was preaching, all of a sudden, a light went on in my head. I said, "Hey, that's what I have been asking God to teach me!" So as he broke for a commercial, I ran into my bedroom to get my copy of the *Expositor's Study Bible*, because he said that the commentary section was written to help the reader better understand the scriptures.

As his program resumed, I started to read along with him that day, and I understood everything that he was saying. This is what my pastors from that little old church in Watts were teaching us. God used them to teach me, by laying for me a foundation for salvation through Jesus's death on the cross. Daily, our pastors lived the word of God before us, and as a result, all the members of that little church, me included, wanted what they had in the Lord: A very close relationship with Jesus Christ and faith that moved mountains. But I had failed initially trying to get it, because I was serving God the wrong way by doing things my way in a ministry that belonged to God in the first place. However, God used Jimmy Swaggart's *Expositor's Study Bible* as a guide, giving me a better understanding of the cross of Jesus Christ that I now understand clearly and live by.

Our pastor from that little old church in Watts, California, have told us over the years on so many occasions from the pulpit: "How can you save anybody when you need saving yourself?"

I now understand what he meant. We have one soul and one lifetime to get it right. He and his wife, our first lady, are both now gone home to be with the Lord, but I can still hear them in my spirit with their brand, like only they can, of righteous teachings. I'm so looking forward to that day when I'll see them again in heaven. They both would tell the congregation, "Read the word of God for yourself, and then, believe every word of it!." The little church in Watts is still going strong, under the leadership of Willie's wife, and their daughter, alongside several members of the Bynum family.

I would like to encourage you to constantly pray, asking God for his help. We cannot make it alone (Philippians 4:6–7).

Pray, and then, pray some more. This curse of sin was passed unto every man from the beginning when Adam disobeyed God (Genesis 2:16–17). So, as a result, death has passed on to every soul that is born into this world. See Romans 5:12, which says all [every male or female born of mankind] are born with this sin nature or with various sin-driven lust [strong desires] to sin. Therefore, the sin nature is nature's way of doing things that no one has to teach us, even as babies. Nature works naturally through our body's flesh to protect and to preserve itself. However, our nature can be led by the spirit of God or led by the lusting of the flesh (Galatians 5:16–17). Both cannot happen at the same time.

I understand that the only way to overcome sin, is by allowing Jesus, being the Word of God, to penetrate my heart and mind (John 15:3). Why? Because this is where the sin nature lives and lies. It is by faith in the finished work of Jesus on the cross which allows the spirit of God to lead and direct me daily. It is the Holy Spirit, according to the scriptures, that leads and guides us all into all truths. I realize that I cannot even tell the truth but by the Holy Spirit, which is the Spirit of truth (John 14:16-17,16:13). Without the guidance of the Holy Spirit, I found myself telling lies all the time. According to the scriptures, a liar is an impure person, and that type of individual will not go to heaven. (Revelation 21:8, 27, and 22:15–16).

The Holy Spirit is the power of God that keeps us drawn into salvation and the work of God (Acts 1:8). God has plans for us and is directing our lives daily if we let him. God wants to be working in our many decisions, situations, and circumstance that arise in our everyday walk (Jeremiah 29:11, 1 Corinthians 12:18, and Luke 24:49). The benefits of the Holy Spirit is the promise of God, according to the following scriptures (Acts 2:1–4 and Joel 2:28–32).

I also learned that only with the working of the Holy Spirit can we make good and true conscious decisions in doing the will of God. Without the help of the Holy Spirit, our consciousness is flawed. For

God's will is his words, and his words are his will. We are to walk in the spirit [the word] and we will not fulfill the lust [evil desires] of the flesh (Galatians 5:16–21; 1 Corinthians 5:9–13, 6:9–11).

As believers, we should not hear the word of God at church and leave it there (Mark 4), but we should implement the word daily in our lives so that it will make the difference (1 Timothy 2:15 and John 15:10). There are signs which should be working in your lives, if you are a believer, and the first sign of being a believer is casting out Devil (Mark 16:15–18).

Why? Because our faith in Christ is the reason why this fight is so great with the Devil (1 Timothy 6:12). And only with our faith in Christ's finish work on the cross and the Holy Spirit's help will we have victory over the schemes of the Devil (Revelations 12:11). If the enemy can take control of our minds, he has our bodies (Romans 12:1 and 2). None of us want Jesus to say, "I never knew you" (Matthew 7:21–23).

What does God accept? Repentance, faith in Jesus, the cross, obedience, and talking to him constantly. Wow, that sounds like a relationship (Luke 9:23–26).

The Fruits of the Spirit. Yes, a relationship in which God has made possible for anyone to have with his son, Jesus. As the relationship with him deepens, without a doubt, one will develop the many attributes (like love or joy) of being a follower or a disciple of his in this relationship. These attributes are referred to as The Fruit of the Spirit. One can't just have one or two of these fruit of the spirit without the others. For these fruit works as one (heart) in God but having 'nine' separate attributes. According to Galatians 5: 22-26, the fruit of the Spirit is love, joy, peace, longsuffering, gentleness, goodness, faith, meekness, temperance: against such there is no law.

After I asked God to forgive me, I also rededicated my heart back to Jesus Christ and again asked him to be my Lord and Savior, and he forgave me of all my sins and gave me a clean heart.

I prayed the Sinner's Prayer: "Dear God in heaven, I am sorry for all my sins, please forgive me of all my sins and come into my heart and be my God. I believe that Jesus is the Christ, and I believe he's your son, and that he came into this world to die on the cross for sin, my sin. God, I believe Jesus's shed blood was for me too. I believe he rose from the dead and now he's sitting on your right side in heaven making intersession for me. Jesus, I accept you as my Lord and Savior. God, I pray this prayer in Jesus's name. Amen" (Romans 10:9–10).

First, I had to be truthful with myself, because if I couldn't tell myself the truth, then I could not be helped or help anyone else, let alone write this book. After much studying; learning—rather, being taught—by God, and still being taught, I accept and believe in all the scriptures that God has given me in this book, which came from the entire Holy Bible. Now, I'm passing them on to you, the reader. I now realized that I was totally serving him the wrong way, as a true born-again believer. I also had to admit that I was persuaded by the Devil [demon spirits]. How? I became a servant to sin by turning away from God's word (Romans 6:12–16). I had made conscious choices, and my choices was not measured by the word of God. My choices caused me to go against God's moral instructions, the Holy Bible, for living a saved and sin-free life (Roman 6:18). When I went against his word in any way, I would give up the redemption power of Jesus's blood and the promise of eternal life through faith. This gave demon spirits the right to oppress me and, ultimately, take over me and possess me. Whatever I chose to do that was not right opened up the door for that particular spirit to enter in and/or rule in my mind, heart, and body and then eventually my life. As a result, I become that thing, acting it out through my flesh, which is called possession.

By then, he [Satan] started giving me his words, and at this point, as a believer in Jesus Christ, I no longer was being led by the Holy Spirit but by demon spirits which only drives us to sin more and more against the Godhead; God the father, God the son, and God the Holy Spirit. (Roman 7)

I did not just only commit sins in (through) the (my) flesh but also spiritual adultery which is when I left my first love, God and Christ (Revelation 2:4–5). How? By finding something or someone else to love instead.

Remember this: Everything that has to do with God and his righteousness points to Jesus being Savior and the Holy Spirit as the drawing power to keep us in the goodness of God. If this is not the case, then willful tendencies will have us go against God and each other in many ways, causing others to fall with us. God will not let us do what we want. He will not let us pervert the things that are holy. Even if it may seem as if things are going good to the eyes. Remember, the Devil can and will offer us things too (Matthew 4:1–4).

Where there is no knowledge of God, there is chaos (Hosea 4:6). We can cause one to sin by the inclusion of or the provoking vices that works through our flesh. God has shown me that anytime I am presented with anything, there is a space of time in the mind before it goes into my heart. I will recognize it as a person, place, or thing first. And, after that, it is also known whether it is a good thing or a bad thing, and the effects it will bring will be identified beforehand. Then, there will come a space in time that a decision has to be made (to do right or wrong) about that person, place, or thing, having learned beforehand the effects of either. At that stage of recognizing what was brought to me, I had to first know what the truth is: the word of God (Psalms 119:142; John 17:17; 1 John 1:8).

If I didn't know what God's word says, then I will always make a choice that seems natural or goes with tradition in the mind. It will seem right to me. In other words, the choices are self-gratification or sensuality, which is the power of human nature to have a desire to please one's flesh [my own personal desires], and most likely, the end result will be giving into my sinful nature. My human nature was given over willfully, voluntarily to my sin nature by my choices. The ungodly desires that lurked in my heart were also in the hearts of those whom I called my friends, my associates (Galatians 5:7–8).

It was so hard to separate from them. But when I began to be obedient to God's word and surrounded myself back with individuals who really wanted to live for God, my salvation walk began to be easier, and it didn't happen overnight. I was fighting daily.

If I would listen, almost always Satan (demons) would start talking to my mind by telling their side of the truth, which was always a lie, to hook me, and it seemed right and okay to do, at least at the time (John 8:44).

And before I could get any release from that lie (thought), two things had to happen: I had to repent and believe that Jesus's death on the cross and his blood took care of all my sins. Again, I prayed in Jesus's name; this time, I am praying against the evil thoughts that would come into my mind and rebuke the evil with the word of God (2 Corinthians 10:5).

Ephesians 6:12 says, "For we wrestle not against flesh and blood, but against principalities, against powers, against the rulers of the darkness of the world, against spiritual wickedness in high places."

As children of God, we cannot live the way we want to. 1 Corinthians 10:21–22 says, "We can't eat from God's table and from the table of devils." As I've stated before, God will leave us; he won't stay.

God cannot dwell where sin is. Please don't get me wrong, the Holy Spirit is not bound and will set free from bondages those whom he will, and he will fill with the Holy Spirit those whom he will. However, when we first give our life to God, we are coming with all kinds of ungodly baggage. I know I did (John 8:11). Jesus told Mary Magdalene to go and sin no more. It doesn't say how much long later after this, but Jesus did cast seven devils out of her in Mark 16:9, but it was only after she got saved. We know her story as a prostitute, and everything that come with that profession is sin.

I mention this because I'm a born-again believer in Christ Jesus, and I let a demon persuade me from living for God, doing all kinds of ungodly things. But while I was on that forty-day fast, God started delivering me from the demon spirits that had me bound. No one laid hands on me to cast them out. I mentioned earlier in the book that my pastors could not pray for me, although I truly believe they did in their private prayer closet. And it was the Holy Spirit delivering me, bringing all those (evil) desires out of my fleshy heart, things that I wasn't proud of.

Now, having understood God's message of why Jesus's death on the cross was so important to me, I just wanted to make sure that I wasn't missing anything, so I repented all over again! It might not have been necessary, but I wanted to make sure (Philippians 3:14). I did so by telling God how sorry I was for sinning against him and the many others that I had hurt throughout my entire life. I prayed that he wouldn't let anyone's blood be on my hands, nor mine on others but that he would save us all. I repeatedly thanked him for forgiving me of all "my" sins. He has put them far away from me and wants me to focus on my new life in Christ (Romans 8).

Hebrews 10:19–27 says: "Having therefore, brethren boldness to enter into the holiest by the blood of Jesus,… By a new and living way, which he hath consecrated for us, through the vail, that is to say, his flesh (Jesus' body)… And having a high priest over the house of God; Let us draw near with a true heart in full assurance of faith, having our hearts sprinkled from an evil conscience, and our bodies washed with pure water." Remember, God told me I missed heaven because "my heart wasn't right", it's a heart thing. (Jeremiah 17:9-10)

The Bible clearly tells us that God did not create hell for his children. Hell was created for the disobedient—the Devil himself (Lucifer), the Devil's angels, and the ungodly individuals (1 Peter 3:19–20; 2 Peter 2:4; and Jude 1:6).

In Luke 16:19–31, it gives an account of what happens once death comes to individuals. And once death comes, you can't stop it nor can your destiny be altered (The only time I remember in scripture of an individual's death time changed was with Hezekiah in 1 Kings 20 and Isaiah 38)

The passage of scripture in Luke talks about two individuals: One is a certain rich man, the other man is Lazarus, a certain beggar. Lazarus was someone whom Jesus called by name.

> There was a certain rich man, which was clothed in purple and fine linen, and fared sumptuously every day:
> And there was a certain beggar named Lazarus, which was laid at his gate, full of sores,
> And desiring to be fed with the crumbs which fell from the rich man's table: moreover, the dogs came and licked his sores.
> And it came to pass, that the beggar died, and was carried by the angels into Abraham's bosom: the rich man also died, and was buried;

> And in hell he lift up his eyes, being in torments, and seeth Abraham afar off, and Lazarus in his bosom.
>
> And he cried and said, Father Abraham, have mercy on me, and send Lazarus, that he may dip the tip of his finger in water, and cool my tongue; for I am tormented in this flame.
>
> But Abraham said, Son, remember that thou in thy lifetime receivedst thy good things, and likewise Lazarus evil things: but now he is comforted, and thou art tormented.
>
> And besides all this, between us and you there is a great gulf fixed: so that they which would pass from hence to you cannot; neither can they pass to us, that would come from thence.
>
> Then he said, I pray thee therefore, father, that thou wouldest send him to my father's house: For I have five brethren; that he may testify unto them, lest they also come into this place of torment.
>
> Abraham said unto him, They have Moses and the prophets; let them hear them.
>
> And he said, Nay, father Abraham: but if one went unto them from the dead, they will repent.
>
> And he said unto him, If they hear not Moses and the prophets, neither will they be persuaded, though one rose from the dead.

I tell you, it is a mystery how God's transformation took place in my mind and heart, by *grace* it did happen. So I say to you, just trust God and believe him for everything. Believe that Jesus paid for all your sins, and the reconciling of your relationship to God were all taken care of on the cross. Whatever your heart is longing for, it is made complete, done.

"It is finished," Jesus said (John 19:30). Jesus died victoriously, and what he came to do was completed on the cross for you, me, and all men, at all times, everywhere. Seek God and just believe (2 Timothy 1:6–13 and 1 Corinthians 10:13).

You see, if a person's mind is closed regarding believing in the entire inspired holy word of God, the Holy Bible, the word of God will always be rejected in the heart. And in his or her mind a belief system is formed. We have to remember that Satan quoted half of the passages of scriptures to Jesus trying to tempt him. But Jesus used the whole entire written passages of scriptures when dealing with Satan (Matthew 4:1–11). Through the power of the holy word of God, the Devil fled, and the angels came to Jesus's aid. Therefore, we must stand on the entire word of God fully, not partially. And when we do, Jesus will send us our help.

I can't put enough emphasis on how we have to believe in our heart that the whole word of God is true and how we must obey every single word written. We cannot take no part of God's word to justify [make it right to do] the thing(s) we lust for in the flesh [the body]. If it is right, call it right, and if it is wrong, call it wrong. If we do not, then we become guilty.

James 2:10 writes, "For whosoever shall keep the whole law, and yet offend in one point, he is guilty of all."

Therefore, we are obliged to keep the entire word of God. And still, that cannot be done without Jesus's help. I found this to be true, and how I've made it these years and how I must keep this same mind to stay in favor with God, I believed everything I have written to you in this book to be truly from God through Jesus Christ my Lord and Savior. And I first believe with all my heart that when Jesus died on that cross so many years ago, he did it for me, too, having all my sins in mind when he was ridiculed and beaten beyond recognition. Enduring those whips was for me (Isaiah 53). I don't mean to sound selfish; however, every man has to claim him for him or herself. But as God showed me through Jesus's life, death, and resurrection, I could have a new mind and a new heart; it became a true personal relationship of true falling in love with my heavenly father and my Jesus. I found more than I ever have before. And they are with me in my salvation walk.

And Jesus went on that cross in my place so that I could have a new start in this lifetime with our heavenly father. My willpower is not strong enough to say, "No," to these sinful desires that would work through my body parts, causing me to sin against God.

My *no's* had me repenting and going back to that sin, repenting and going back, which left me broken and with a heart full of regrets, hating myself, and not forgiving myself, because I felt so unworthy as a child of God. But, truly, I wanted God to find something in me he could use (Matthew 7:16–20).

Since my willpower was and is so weak, I believed that Jesus overcame all things, big and small, for me on that cross. So then, once again, I started directing all those evil desires that had formed in my heart, all flashbacks of sin, and the hard situations that was caused or the residue of them. I began to speak it all out to God in praying. I spoke out everything. I went back as far as to the sins of my youth that would come to my mind or I could remember. And this is what I said to God and meant it with all my heart, because I just didn't know what else to say:

> Father God of Heaven, creator of all things, Father of My Lord and Savior Jesus Christ who is your only begotten Son, I also claim.
>
> God, please, let Jesus's life, death, and resurrection do what you have said in your word it is supposed to do for me. God I cannot help myself. I need your help. I believe that through Jesus death on the cross I have been given by you God the power to say no to these desires that keeps coming back to lure me, to entice me, because I'm choosing to say "yes" to you and obeying your holy word. I love you both, and I want to live right. I want to keep your word and keep my word to you by loving you and keeping your commandments. God, please keep me, guide me, and teach me all your ways. I want to

see your face in peace. I don't want to go to that
place you have shown me God. Amen.

Ever since I have prayed that prayer, the results that have followed I know nobody but God the father has done. I know he will continue to make good things happen in my life. That does not mean I don't have problems, those come. I now know how I can pray, and I believe that he's going to send me an answer, and an answer comes every time. He hasn't failed me yet, and I know he never will. He's God, my God.

God wants us to keep all his words. He's the only one that knows how to get us into heaven (John 14:6). If we knew how, we wouldn't need a Savior. Jesus simply says in John 14:15: "If you love me, keep my commandments."

Verse 21 says, "He who has my commandments, and keeps them, he it is who loves me: and he who loves me shall be loved of my father, and I will love him, and will manifest myself to him."

In August 2012, I still found myself asking God to please let this book be penned by him. "Nothing is to be of me Lord, please," I prayed. "And please don't be angry at my asking you so many times."

And that same night, as I was studying God's word looking up a scripture, my Bible page flipped, and my eyes fell on this passage of scripture: Habakkuk 2:1–4. I read it and was as shocked as how God right then confirmed his word by telling me in the scripture. If he did it for him, he will do it for me. I couldn't remember ever seeing this passage in the Bible before. I said to myself, *I thought I read the Bible through, but I don't remember this.*

Habakkuk 2:1–4 writes, I will stand upon my watch, and set me upon the tower, and will watch to see what He will say unto me, and what I shall answer when I am reproved. And the LORD answered me, and said, Write the vision, and make it plain upon tables, that he may run who reads it. For the vision is yet for an appointed time, but at the end it shall speak, and not lie: though it tarry, wait for it; because it will surely come, it will not tarry. Behold, his soul which is lifted up is not upright in him: but the just shall live by his Faith."

Oh, how my heart was relieved, and I felt good, joyful. I could have burst with joy, if it was such a thing, because all I ever want is to obey God and, in the end, see his face in peace. He is the only living God; he gave me so many chances, and that's what I call having his grace. And not only did God forgive my failures, he gave me a new start so many years ago, showing me that his love for me is more than my little mind could ever imagine. He also told me that all of my praying and crying out to him, wanting this book to be his words of my testimony, was heard. Then, he opened my mind to see that the writing of this book is not in vain. So I thank God, and I give him all the praise and glory for allowing Jesus to manifest himself to me.

Finally, I have done what God have asked. His grace is sufficient and amazing (2 Corinthians 12:9).

Although it has been so many years of hardships and struggles to write, finish, and to proofread the book, now my heart is at peace with God: it is done. God have not shown me the vision since 1994. However, I relive it every time I get to tell it. I have accomplished what God has asked me to do in 1995. He told me:

"Write it down, put it in a book, and tell my people, tell my churches, that…HELL…IT IS REAL!"

My Vision of Hell: A Sacrifice for Others to See

"God showed me hell, a fiery place of judgment, torment, and a lake of fire for the ungodly (Revelation 20:15) then brought me back to tell about it."

Thank you for taking the time to read about My Vision of Hell! I would like to invite you, if needed to pray the following pray ensuring your salvation. Again thanks, and May God Bless you.

Sinners Prayer

God, I come to you in the name of your son Jesus.
I admit that I am a sinner. I believe that Jesus
died on the cross for my sins, and I believe
in my heart that you raised Him from the
dead so that I can be saved.

Jesus, I invite you to come into my heart
and be the Lord of my life from this day
forward.

Lord God, thank you for saving me.
I pray this prayer in Jesus name…
Amen.

These are some Bible Scriptures teaching on hell fire:

Deuteronomy 32:22
2 Samuel 22:6
Job 11:8
Job 26:6
Psalms 9:17, 16:10, 55:15, and 139:8
Proverbs 5:5, 7:27, 9:18, 15:11 and 24, 23:14, and 27:20
Isaiah 5:14, 14:9, and 28:15 and 18
Ezekiel 31:16 and 32:21
Jonah 2:2
Habakkuk 2:5
Matthew 5:22, 29, and 30; 13:49-50; 10:28; 11:23; 16:18; 23:15 and 33; 25:30
Mark 9:42–48
Luke 10:15 and 16:23
Acts 2:27 and 2:31
James 3:6
1 Peter 3:19–20
2 Peter 2:4
Jude 1:6
Revelation 1:18, 6:8, 19:20, 20:10–15, and 21:8

About the Author

Sheila M. Drummer was born in 1963 in James Mill, AR, where she was raised. She moved to Los Angeles with her family where she graduated from Lynwood Unified School District. She is blessed to be married to her husband of 37 years. Through their union, they have seven children and seventeen grandchildren.

In 1995 Sheila was called to the ministry in a small church in Watts, CA, where she served with sincere dedication. When the church expanded in 1996, it was God who told Sheila and her family to move to Bakersfield in order to support what would become known as Greater Lighthouse Community Outreach, Inc. In December of 1998, Sheila was ordained and appointed as Assistant Pastor to the Youth Ministry of Greater Lighthouse (dba The Blessing Corner Ministries) where she still serves today. For the past twenty-two years, she has ministered the love of Jesus Christ to the lives of thousands of children, adults and seniors.

CPSIA information can be obtained
at www.ICGtesting.com
Printed in the USA
BVHW081920260423
662928BV00002B/6